C0-ARQ-363

ARCHAEOLOGY IN CHINA

General Editor
WILFRID J. MILLINGTON SYNGE

ARCHAEOLOGY IN CHINA

WILLIAM WATSON

with 146 illustrations in halftone

MAX PARRISH · LONDON

MAX PARRISH & CO LTD
55 QUEEN ANNE STREET, LONDON W.1

PRINTED AND MADE IN GREAT BRITAIN BY
FLETCHER & SON LTD NORWICH AND
THE LEIGHTON-STRAKER BOOKBINDING CO LTD LONDON

ACKNOWLEDGMENTS

The illustrations in this book have been selected from an exhibition of photographs of some of the most important archaeological discoveries of the last ten years sent to Britain by the Chinese Society for Cultural Relations with Foreign Countries and exhibited under the auspices of the Britain-China Friendship Association to whom we are indebted for permission to reproduce. The exhibition opened at the University of London Institute of Archaeology in November 1958 and subsequently toured the country with great success.*

The objects reproduced are not equally representative for every period and type, either in variety or quality; but the fact of their being documented as to find place, mutual association and other particulars makes their historical value greater than that of many outstanding finds which lack such information.

W.J.M.S.

* With the exception of Plates 9b, 10 and 33a, which illustrate material exchanged against British specimens between the Archaeological Institute of the Chinese Academy of Sciences and the British Museum; and Plates 53 and 56, which illustrate other pieces in the collection of the British Museum.

Key to the Sites Shown on the Map

ANYANG 9
CANTON 26
CH'ANG SHA 21
CHENG CHOU 10
CHIA KO CHUANG 20
CHOUKOUTIEN 1
ERH LI KANG 11
HAI TAO YING TZŬ TS'UN 15
HSIN TSAO HSIANG 23
HSING LUNG HSIEN 19
HUA T'ING TS'UN 6
LIANG CHU 7
LIU LI KO 12
LOYANG 28
LUNG SHENG KANG 25
PAI TAO KOU P'ING 4
PAN PO TS'UN 3
PEI CHAI TS'UN 24
P'U TU TS'UN 17
SHIH CHAI SHAN 27
SHIH CHIA HO 5
SHOU HSIEN 18
TA SSŬ K'UNG TS'UN 13
T'AN SHIH SHAN 8
TING TS'UN 2
WANG TU HSIEN 22
WU KUAN TS'UN 14
YEN TUN SHAN 16

INTRODUCTION

A generation ago western archaeologists were already able to present a picture of prehistoric and early historic cultures in Europe and the Near East which had some semblance of unity and continuity. The early literate cultures of Egypt and Mesopotamia led on to the archaic and classical cultures of Crete and Greece. Even the Neolithic, stone-using communities of wilder Europe in the north and west were brought into the orbit of civilization diffusing from the Mediterranean. Polished stone tools often seem to be imitations of the bronze tools of more advanced contemporaries. The techniques of food-production itself, grain growing and cattle-raising, were spread by migrant farmers who had been in contact with more populous and more inventive communities. The historical unity embraced the high Bronze-Age cultures of the Mediterranean and the Near East at the centre, passed into an aura of Neolithic cultures which felt their influence and borrowed from them, and ended in a penumbra of increasing savagery and technological simplicity.

The discovery in recent years of the remains of bronze-age river valley civilizations in India and China, comparable in technical knowledge and social development, though not in age, to the ancient civilizations of the Nile and Euphrates, aroused western curiosity in the question of ultimate historical relations of East and West: did India and the Far East receive their knowledge of food-production from the same source as the Near East, or was the invention repeated independently? Was knowledge of bronze metallurgy conveyed from the Near East (where its priority is still unquestioned) to China, or did the Chinese make the revolutionary discovery for themselves? Relations between the Indus Valley civilization and Mesopotamia could be readily imagined but the passage of very specific techniques from west to east across the thinly populated steppes and highlands of Asia seemed more problematic.

It was recognized that both in the late Neolithic of north-west China and in the Bronze-Age material from the Central Plain, some degree of contact with far-western techniques and forms must be admitted. Some western orientalists interpreted these signs of contact as the result of ethnic migrations, the transfer over vast distances of more or less complete cultural complexes. In this they were influenced perhaps by the study of cultural movements of the Neolithic and Bronze Age of Europe. Here some well-defined cultures, each possessed of some superiority of equipment or organization, may be traced in their migration through and to areas of comparatively more savage population. The Bronze-Age cultures of eastern Europe, of northern Asia east of the Urals and even of southern Siberia have enough in common to suggest that they, like the Bronze Age of western and northern Europe, owed their existence to the diffusion of a single great tradition, the ultimate source of which must be the high civilizations of the Near East. It seemed possible that China too had benefited from the same cultural diffusion, which must originate in the 'Fertile Crescent' of the Near East, and have been transmitted by peoples migrating in search of a new home. For it was clear that the civilization of Bronze-Age China was superior to any other which has left its traces through Asia east of the Caucasus.

Before the late war some intensive field work had been carried out in Chinese archaeology, notably the excavations at Anyang on the site of the Shang dynasty capital, conducted by Li Chi for the Academia Sinica; and at Choukoutien Pei and Black had made the first discovery in China of Palaeolithic human remains and implements. Licent and de Chardin made the first systematic investigation of the stone-age sites in the Ordos region. Andersson's collecting of painted funeral urns in Kansu laid the basis of the study of the Neolithic in the north-west; and by its excavations at Ch'eng-tzŭ-Yai the archaeologists of Academia Sinica had shown the existence of a separate Neolithic tradition in the north-west which shows signs of intimate connexion with the Shang Bronze Age. In 1948 Wu Gin-ding published a pioneering work in the analysis of the Neolithic potteries. The work of Finn on islands near Hong Kong revealed a Neolithic tradition, recognized as comparatively late in date, which is distinct from both the northern traditions.

But it is no exaggeration to say that only the last ten years of wide-spread excavation and surveying conducted by the Archaeological Institute of the Academy of Sciences (founded by the Communist government in 1949) has filled out our picture of the prehistoric and early dynastic material cultures of China to an extent approaching our knowledge of comparable cultures in the west and Near East. Mr Hsia Nai, Deputy Director of the Archaeological Institute, has continued work at Anyang, carrying out major excavations at Hui Hsien and other sites. Provincial museums, such as that of Nanking under the energetic guidance of its keeper Mme Tseng Chao-yüeh, have excavated on chosen sites and made regional surveys. Throughout China the Committees for the Administration of Cultural Properties (part of the local organization of the Ministry of Culture) have surveyed, excavated and rescued sites and material continuously since their establishment in 1950. As a result the culture of the Yellow River is revealed as no less an independent, self-nurtured phenomenon than the civilizations centred on the great rivers of the Near East. It is reasonable to suppose that, in Neolithic times as in the Bronze Age, the Central Plain of China was a generative centre from which influence radiated outwards, although further research is needed to establish the truth of this, and to determine how far Chinese influence spread to the north-west and through Asia to meet influences passing eastwards from the Near East. The expansion of Chinese culture in Han times into Korea, Indo-China and the mountainous south-western provinces of Szechwan and Yünnan is a chapter of recorded history which archaeological research can illustrate. The influence of China in the formation of the art of the Steppe nomads and the nature of the relation between Central China and South Siberia are questions which future discoveries may resolve more fully, though these connexions are already recognizable. The acceptance of certain culture-traits from the far west is also undeniable: the knowledge of bronze-casting itself must have travelled eastwards from the Near East as the germ of a technological and social revolution; but in the forms which the bronze was used to produce, and in art, the culture of the Chinese city states as a whole is an individual growth.

Palaeolithic

The sparseness of our information simplifies the picture of the Palaeolithic period. As far as is known at present the earliest traces of human activity in Asia proper, i.e. east of the Urals and north of the Himalayas, are those discovered from 1921 onwards in clefts in limestone hills situated 26 miles south-west of Peking at the now famous site of Choukoutien. Here were found the remains of numerous individuals of a type designated Peking Man, together with roughly worked stone tools. The latter differ in form and technique of manufacture from the 'hand-axes' characteristic of the early Palaeolithic of western Europe, but they are of comparable antiquity, perhaps half a million years old. At another point of the Choukoutien site ('Locality 15') were found stone implements made of finer material – a smooth-textured flint – in which there are signs of technological advance even when allowance is made for the greater ease of working in the new material. The most important recent discovery of Palaeolithic remains, at Ting Ts'un, belongs approximately to the same period (the later part of the Lower Palaeolithic, corresponding roughly to the Acheulian of Europe) and to the same technological stage.

The period which intervenes between this Palaeolithic age and the rise of Neolithic cultures in China is poorly represented in the archaeological record. We must assume a degree of continuity in the human population, if only because of physical characteristics encountered in Peking Man (the 'shovel-shaped' incisor is the chief of these) which survive in the Chinese population to the present time.

Sites with the small stone tools called microliths are found widespread in Manchuria, where they are often combined with Neolithic elements in the form of polished or partly polished stone axes, crude hand-made pots with rounded or pointed bases and simple impressed or incised decoration, and small triangular arrowheads of flint. These traits of Neolithic culture probably indicate the radiating influence of the advanced Neolithic culture of the Central Plain. The mixture of Palaeolithic or Mesolithic traits with features derived from the Neolithic is appropriate to a region lying on the fringes of a centre of settled farming economy, and repeats a phenomenon which may be observed also in prehistoric Europe.

Neolithic

In north China archaeological finds from the beginning of the Neolithic period onwards are abundant. Since 1949, when systematic regional surveying and publication was undertaken by the present authorities, it has been possible to interpret the signs of cultural advance and regional interaction on the lines pioneered by the prehistoric archaeologists of Europe and the U.S.S.R.

The outline given below resumes the barest facts of classification. It is a fault of this classification that it rests mainly on distinctions of fine pottery traditions which need not – and in many particulars it can be shown that they do not – correspond to other fundamental features of a cultural complex, such as the distribution of the coarse pottery types, the shapes of tools, methods of building houses and burying the dead. Methods of classification appropriate to the relatively isolated Neolithic communities of prehistoric Europe are less satisfactorily applied to a flat, fertile, populous region which lacks any considerable natural barriers to cultural and economic intercommunication.

There are three main divisions of Neolithic Culture in China:

1. The Painted Pottery Cultures (Pan Shan and Yang-shao Cultures).
2. The Black Pottery Culture (Lung Shan Culture).
3. The South-east Neolithic.

1. *The Painted Pottery Cultures* (Kansu Neolithic and Yang-shao Cultures).

A painted pottery tradition is found in north-west and central China. Two main divisions can be distinguished, both associated with a Neolithic economy.

Along the river valleys of Kansu Province are found burials accompanied by pots of buff ware, some of them apparently finished on a turning device. They are burnished and decorated with formal patterns in black and crimson paint. The most striking and probably the oldest of them are the large urns of the Pan Shan culture. They have a general resemblance to the painted jars of the Caucasian Bronze Age, as excavated at Trialeti, and they demonstrate a western influence, possibly with some contact of population.

In central China, especially in south Honan and south Shansi, is found a distinct variety of painted pottery, which is named after the type-site at Yang-shao in south-west Honan. The Yang-shao pottery includes a characteristic shallow bowl with painted decoration on the lip and inside; it sometimes has a white slip and lacks the tall urns of Kansu and the decorative patterns associated with these. The coarse pottery found at Yang-shao sites in central China is grey and undecorated; it includes the tripod vessels called *ting* and the vessel with three-lobed base called *li*, and belongs to a tradition which survived far into the Bronze Age.

The chronological and geographical relationship of the Pan Shan and Yang-shao cultures is not yet clear; it has recently been shown that sites of Yang-shao type occur farther west than was expected, even in Kansu itself. A further variety of painted pottery found in Kansu, designated Ma-Ch'ang, is similar to that of Pan Shan, but coarser, and appears to mark a later stage of the Pan Shan culture.

2. *The Black Pottery Culture* (Lung Shan Culture)

Ch'eng Tz'ŭ Yai in Shantung is the type-site of a north-eastern Neolithic tradition, with which is associated a black pottery often called after Lung Shan, the name of a nearby town. The finest variety of this ware is thin-walled and burnished black or dark-brown, and has been turned on a wheel. The pots have angular profiles suggestive of metal or turned wooden vessels. No metal was in fact found with the black burnished ware at Chʻeng Tzʻŭ Yai, but the practice there of oracle-taking by cracking bone with heat suggests a connexion with the earliest known bronze culture of China, that of the Shang dynastic period, which flourished in north and south-east Honan from about the 15th to the 11th century B.C. Several sites in north Honan show a sequence of painted Yang-shao ware, followed by Lung Shan black ware, and again by the grey pottery of the Shang period.

The exact limits of the Lung Shan culture, as defined by the thin polished pottery, are not yet clear; but it does not seem to occur west of Honan, or commonly south of Shantung. Lung Shan coarse ware includes two varieties of the three-lobed vessel called *li*, and in general it resembles the coarse ware found at the Yang-shao sites of Honan.

3. *The South-east Neolithic*

A third Neolithic tradition is represented by sites in the south-eastern provinces of Fukien and Kuantung, especially near the coast and along the river valleys. Its characteristic pottery is a hard light grey or brown ware, hand-made, and decorated with impressed geometric patterns, or patterns resembling basket-work. The people of this south-east Neolithic depended more on hunting and fishing than the agricultural and cattle-rearing communities of the Painted and Black Pottery cultures. The tradition lasted almost until the Han period. Its beginnings cannot be dated; it may not go back farther than the Shang period – the second half of the second millennium B.C. In the coastal provinces of Chekiang and Kiangsu, where the influence of the south-east Neolithic extended, subsisted other local traditions perhaps remotely connected with the Lung Shan culture.

The Bronze Age

The Shang dynasty culture as revealed in excavations near Anyang, in the north of Honan province, is already possessed of an advanced art of bronze-casting, comparable technically with that of the late Bronze Age of Europe. The earliest known stage of this craft is seen at Erh-Li-Kang and Liu-Li-Ko, but it does not fall far behind the average standard practised at Anyang. The sudden appearance in China of accomplished metallurgy might indicate that the main elements of Shang culture came to China from outside in an already developed form, or that an 'Early Bronze Age' which has so far eluded archaeologists must still be sought for. But in recent years it has become increasingly clear that a third view must be entertained: while it seems undeniable that the knowledge of bronze casting came to China from the west, this need not imply that any considerable culture came with it. Bronze seems from the start in China to have been used with astonishing skill to cast vessels decorated with animal and geometric patterns which had already reached an evolved stage in wood or bone carving. Nevertheless among the bronze artifacts traits linking with the west are present. A form of spearhead, the socketed axe, animal-headed knives (a speciality of South Siberia) and perhaps some chariot parts – possibly the general design of the chariot itself – are items clearly owed to foreign influence.

It was the custom in Shang times to consult gods on crops, rain, military campaigns, and the royal comings and goings, by interpreting cracks formed in the shoulder-bones of animals and in tortoise-shell by applying a hot point. Frequently the questions, and sometimes the answers, were inscribed on the bone. From the all-important questions about sacrifices to ancestral spirits (e.g. 'will such-and-such a sacrifice be acceptable to so-and-so?') the list of Shang kings has been reconstructed. It is found to correspond almost exactly with the list preserved in history. Thus is confirmed the founding of the capital near Anyang by King P'an Keng, whom history reports to have moved there from farther east. The orthodox chronology of Chinese historians dated this move to 1300 B.C., and the end of the dynasty, after the victory of the Chou, to 1122 B.C. Many historians agree however in lowering the latter date to 1027 B.C., which is accepted here in dating the earlier finds. The date of the beginning of the Shang period remains doubtful.

The site of the Shang capital near Anyang at the village of Hsiao T'un was the scene of excavations by the Academia Sinica from 1927 to 1936, and the work was resumed by the Academy of Sciences of Peking in 1950. The civilization of Shang is broadly reminiscent of the city states of the Bronze Age in the Near East: a king, due to be deified after death, ruler in a kind of theocracy; holocausts of human victims at royal funerals, pillared palaces, walls built of stamped earth, carving of hard stone (jade) and rudimentary sculpture, an armament based on the chariot and the bow, some form of slavery (possibly recruited only from prisoners of war), and a system of writing which combines ideographic and phonetic principles.

The excellence of its metal craft is the most distinctive feature of Shang culture. It is seen at its best in the vessels used for sacrifice to gods and ancestors, and which were buried in the graves of great persons. They begin a tradition which persisted through several stylistic transformations until the Han period. The skilled combination of shape and ornament, the high aesthetic quality of the concepts and the execution, constitute one of the outstanding arts of the ancient world, narrow in range of expression but astonishingly powerful. The technical virtuosity found in the best examples is hardly equalled in any other early school of bronze craft. The motifs are dragons and the monster-mask called *t'ao t'ieh*, a few other conventionalized animal forms and some simple geometric units of pattern. The trend of ornament is towards linear elaboration, with spirals and the sudden change of direction in curving lines. Despite the mythological character of the figurative motifs, this is an animal art, based on the fantastic and abstracted treatment of recognizable, though unreal, animal forms. In the development of themes the parts of the form break up, are separated and reconstituted into fresh units of design whose origin is not always immediately apparent. This tendency is in the spirit of the later animal art of the Asiatic steppes, though in ancient China it is carried further. In the earlier stage of the art, in the Shang dynasty and early Chou dynasty, there is no interlacery in the linear pattern – this seems almost deliberately avoided. It appears from about the 8th century B.C. onwards, and from the same period the units of design are increasingly abstract and geometric. Examples of this tradition of ornament will be found in the plates of this book.

The ornament has been subjected to intensive stylistic and chronological study. This aspect of the ancient bronzes however has received close attention only during the last thirty years. But for centuries past, at least from the time of the Sung dynasty, catalogues of bronze vessels have been compiled and the inscriptions which appear on the vessels have been studied with a view to interpreting them in terms of the modern script and so to dating them to their dynasty and extracting historical information. The majority of the inscriptions record briefly the occasion of casting them, or at least the ceremonial name of the ancestor in sacrifices to whom they were to be used. In the early Chou period the presentation of vessels (or the value-equivalent for their manufacture) by feudal rulers to their inferiors in the hierarchy became an official ceremonial symbolizing the efficacy of the feudal ties. In these cases the inscriptions often have great historical importance.

The chief ritual vessels are classified as follows:

Food Vessels

For cooking:	Li (Pl. 41)	Hsien (Pls. 58, 81)
	Ting (Pls. 56, 62, 77)	
Containers:	Kuei (Pls. 60, 63b, 75)	Yü (Pls. 61, 63a)
	Tou (Pl. 85)	Tui (Pls. 74, 88)

Wine Vessels

Containers:	Tsun (Pl. 51)	Hu (Pls. 71, 80, 86)
	Yu (Pls. 50, 57)	Lei (Pl. 68)
Goblets:	Chüeh (Pl. 43)	Ku (Pls. 44, 52)
		Chia (Pl. 42)
For heating and mixing:	Ho (Pls. 66, 69)	
	Kuang (Pl. 65)	

Water Vessels

Basins:	P'an (Pls. 59, 64b)	Yi (Pl. 87)
	Chien (Pl. 73)	

In 1027 B.C. an invasion eastwards by the Chou from their home in Shansi overthrew the Shang rule. Chou armies marched to the eastern seaboard, and as far south as Kiangsu Province. Feudatory states were established throughout the country and Chou ruled at the centre, with its capital at Loyang. The ties between Chou and the vassal states soon proved formal rather than effective. The history of China until the unification of the whole country by Shih Huang Ti in 232 B.C. is one of almost continual struggle between the states in varying alliances. Ch'u in the south became predominant, as did Ch'i in the north, then both succumbed before the eastward expansion of Ch'in, which in 232 B.C. brought the whole country under a single ruler.

The Chou introduced changes in the shapes and decoration of the bronze ritual vessels. From the start a number of styles appear which suggest an artistic tradition distinct from that of the Shang. From about 600 B.C. it is possible to discuss traditions characteristic of certain regions, such as are represented by the bronze vessels of the state of Yen and the style characteristic of the state of Ch'u.

The last few centuries of the Chou period, although we have placed them here in the Bronze Age, saw the introduction of iron and its increasing use in everyday life. A strange contrast with the history of iron metallurgy in Europe is the fact that in China casting was the earlier and always the commoner process, whereas in Europe iron was wrought for almost two thousand years before casting was adopted. Iron was cast in China from about 600 B.C. Perhaps because it was impossible to produce a tough and sharp cutting edge in a mould, bronze was in the main used for weapons until the 3rd century B.C., although tools and even casting moulds of elaborate form could be produced in the new metal. The forging of iron, and the development of iron working generally, are believed to have been among the reasons for the political dominance achieved by the western mountain state of Ch'in towards the end of the Chou period, an ascendancy which culminated in the unification of China under Shih Huang Ti. The ferocity of the Ch'in armies, armed with long iron swords and cutting off heads by the thousand, spread terror through the central and eastern states.

The Han Period

Historical texts which record or purport to record the events of the Shang dynasty and the earlier part of the Chou dynasty offer such dim outlines of the political life of those remote times that the evidence of archaeological remains and of the inscriptions found on bronzes is of major importance in reconstructing the course of history. From the middle of the Chou period onwards however archaeological research assumes the character of 'historical archaeology': the knowledge of material culture derived from the study of excavated relics becomes a part of a fuller picture of ancient life recorded in reliable historical texts. So far comparatively little excavation has taken place on the deserted sites of the capitals of city states, whose vicissitudes of growth and destruction it may in future be possible to relate to historical and military events in the manner demonstrated by European archaeologists in the case of iron-age citadels and Roman military camps and towns. There are greater obstacles in China than in Europe to this kind of archaeological research in the fact that fewer ancient city and fortress sites came to be abandoned: their remains lie beneath cities which have subsisted to the present day. For the present our knowledge of the material life of both late Chou and Han times is derived almost wholly from the excavation of tombs, which are often of elaborate construction and richly furnished with grave goods.

The transition in China from the later Chou period to the Han period offers analogies both in material and intellectual life to the transformation of the western world which occurred between the age of the Greek city states and the establishment of the Roman empire. The age of independent and aggressive small states of the 5th – 3rd centuries B.C., the age also of the intellectual rebirth of which Confucius, Mencius and Laotze are the representatives best known to the west, was replaced by the centralized political structure and cultural uniformity of the Han state. In the crafts there are parallels to be drawn with the factory-like organization of potters and bronzesmiths in imperial Rome. There are exotic elements in the art of Han, particularly in new conventions of depicting animals and landscape, which stand out against traditional motifs inherited from the Chou period. The new themes indicate contacts with the art of steppe nomads and, possibly, at several removes, with Hellenistic art.

Recent excavations have been particularly fortunate in finds illustrating the progress of the major arts in Han times. The murals in the great tomb at Wang Tu are the finest example so far recovered of the figure painting of the period; architectural construction and ornament are exemplified in the monolithic subterranean chambers of the tomb at Pei Chai Ts'un; building in brick with true arches, vaulted and domed roofs is illustrated from a number of large tombs of the 1st and 2nd centuries A.D. The hundreds of Han graves excavated in all parts of the country have produced great numbers of the clay figurines and house models which give so lively an impression of the Han life, and at their best have considerable sculptural merit. Lacquered ware from the government factories has been found in excellent preservation in graves dug in the damp, sandy soil at Ch'ang Sha in Hunan Province.

KEY TO THE SITES AND PLATES

PALAEOLITHIC AND NEOLITHIC
(*Neolithic c.* 2500 – *c.* 500 B.C.)

Ting Ts'un	*Pls.* 1–5
Pan Po Ts'un	6–10
Pai Tao Kou P'ing	11–16a
Shih Chia Ho	16b–21
Hua T'ing Ts'un	22–26
Liang Chu	27–31
T'an Shih Shan	32
Jih Chao	33

BRONZE AGE I: THE SHANG DYNASTY
(16*th century* B.C. – 1027 B.C.)

Erh Li Kang	34–40
Liu Li Ko	41–44
Ta Ssŭ K'ung Ts'un	45–52
Wu Kuan Ts'un	54–55

BRONZE AGE II: EARLIER PERIOD OF THE CHOU DYNASTY
(1027 B.C. – 700 B.C.)

Hai Tao Ying Tzŭ	57–62
Yen Tun Shan	63–66
P'u Tu Ts'un	67–69

BRONZE AGE III: LATER PERIOD OF THE CHOU DYNASTY
(700 B.C. – 223 B.C.)

Shou Hsien	70–77
Hsing Lung Hsien	78
Liu Li Ko, Chao Ku, Ku Wei Ts'un	79–84
Chia Ko Chuang	85–88

THE CH'IN AND HAN PERIODS
(*resp.* 223 – 206 B.C., 206 B.C. – A.D. 220)

Ch'ang Sha	89–97
Wang Tu Hsien	98–105
Hsin Tsao Hsiang	106–109
Pei Chai Ts'un	110–114
Lung Sheng Kang	115–117
Western Suburb, Loyang	118–119
Eastern Suburb, Canton	120–121
Shih Chai Shan	122–123

NOTES ON THE PLATES

PLATES 1–5 Ting Ts'un, Hsiang Fen Hsien, Shansi Province. (*Excavated* 1954.)

A discovery made in 1954 near Ting Ts'un in Shansi Province adds to our knowledge of the Palaeolithic of China. Chert tools and three human teeth were recovered from a gravel bed belonging to a series widely distributed in north China, and lying directly under the loess (Pl. 5). This position corresponds to the period during which the filling of the fissures of the famous site of Choukoutein was accumulated.

The combination of species seen in the animal bones found in the Ting Ts'un gravel suggests a time intervening between the two periods of human occupation at Choukoutien, i.e. between the earlier locality 1 and the later locality 15, and closer to the second (Pl. 3).

The human teeth (one incisor and two molars) from Ting Ts'un are intermediate between those of *Sinanthropus* and modern man. The shovel-shaped formation of the inner face of the incisor – typical of *Sinanthropus* – still remains.

The stone tools from Ting Ts'un repeat the signs of technical advance which appear at locality 15. They include some thick points, of triangular section and about six inches long, superficially like the hand-axes of western Europe but not so well shaped (Pl. 4). The majority of the pieces are neatly struck flakes with retouch on the edge at one side. The shape of the flakes is generally narrower measured in the direction of the flaking than it is in width. There are, however, a number of long flakes and, like the similar pieces from locality 15, these sometimes show signs of preparatory trimming on the core in the manner of the Levalloisian technique of the West (Pl. 5a, b).

The stone tools from Ting Ts'un resemble those of the Late Lower and Middle Palaeolithic of Europe, and the gravel bed in which they were preserved belongs to the later Middle Pleistocene division of geology. Their age may be between 200,000 and 100,000 years.

Ref.: Kuo Mo-jo, Pei Wen-chung *et al.*: *The Discovery and Study of Human Fossils Found in China*, 1955.*

PLATES 6–10 Pan Po Ts'un, near Hsi-an, Shensi Province. (*Excavated* 1954.)

This is the first Neolithic settlement to have been exhaustively excavated in China. Round and oblong hut foundations were uncovered, lying a few feet below the ancient land surface. The timbers of the huts had all perished, but the soil had preserved many traces of post-holes (in the course of excavation these holes were left surrounded by columns of earth) and from them the form of the huts could be inferred to some extent. The round huts were supported at the centre by four pillars spaced around a central hearth (*cf.* Pl. 7). The roof was probably conical, the eaves reaching almost to the ground at the sides, where they rested on small posts set close together. The clay debris found strewn on the floor of most of the huts is believed to have been the covering of the roof, whose timbers had disappeared without trace. In Pl. 8, at the farther side of the round hut foundation, can be seen traces of two light partition walls leading from the entrance, which are another indication of

* NOTE ON THE BIBLIOGRAPHICAL REFERENCES. *K'ao Ku Hsüeh Pao* (Journal of Archaeology), *Wen Wu Ts'an K'ao Tzŭ Liao* (Materials for Cultural History, now called *Wen Wu*), and *K'ao Ku T'ung Hsün* (Archaeological Communications, now called *K'ao Ku*) are the three main archaeological periodicals. The titles of excavation reports and other studies which appear as separate volumes are quoted here in translation.

the conical structure of the roof. Storage spaces, ovens and pottery kilns were formed inside the hut by excavating in the soil. They can be seen lining two walls of the larger rectangular building shown in Plate 6b. The deep pits shown in Pl. 8 were used for storing grain. They are a constant feature of the Neolithic settlements of both Yang-shao and Lung Shan tradition. The huts revealed in the excavations were not all standing at one time, for their floors were found to overlap. But it is clear that the houses stood close together in a compact village.

The pottery is mostly light red in colour, of finely levigated clay, and typical of the superior ware found on Yang-shao Neolithic sites. Nevertheless the pottery vessels in the aggregate are different in character from the typical Yang-shao ware of Honan, where the culture is best known. The curvilinear patterns painted on the sides of bowls in Honan also appear here, but one bowl is decorated with two drawings which are unparalleled in central China, and still remain distinct from the decoration of the painted pottery of Kansu (Pls. 13–16a). These are a human face and a fish (*cf.* Pl. 9a; the fish is on the near side of the interior) done in a geometric style in black paint. The painting of the everted bowl lip follows the Honan custom. The amphora shown on Pl. 10a is peculiar to the Shensi sites.

Ref. *K'ao Ku T'ung Hsün*, 1955.3.7; 1956.2.23; 1957.5.95.

PLATES 11–16a Pai Tao Kou P'ing, Kansu Province. (*Excavated* 1955.)

The district around Lanchou, in the upper course of the Yellow River, was comparatively densely populated by the Neolithic farmers who bequeathed to posterity the fine painted pottery urns which have reached the museums of the world since the beginning of the century. Very few of the tombs which contain the urns have been systematically investigated. The tomb shown in Pl. 11 at the conclusion of excavation is one of a group of 21 discovered by archaeologists charged with the supervision of ancient sites encountered in railway works in Kansu. The disposition of the grave, with the body laid on the right side, legs flexed and head to the east, facing a row of pots in which offerings of grain and meat had been placed, follows a custom peculiar to the north-east province of the painted-pottery Neolithic culture.

All the pottery belongs to the type called Ma Ch'ang, a coarser descendant of the earlier ware, which is termed Pan Shan after the name of a cemetery site. The painting is in purplish black and dark red, in patterns which are for the most part simplified versions of those used on the earlier urns. The dog-tooth band on the neck of the amphora in Pl. 14 has been called the 'death pattern' in the belief that it was applied only to funeral urns. Since no habitation sites of this culture have yet been excavated we do not however know what difference there was between everyday pottery and the vessels made for grave offerings. The vessel shown in Pl. 12 looks like a domestic pot.

Ref.: *Wen Wu Ts'an K'ao Tzŭ Liao*, 1955.5.110.

PLATES 16b–21 Shih Chia Ho, T'ien Mien Hsien, Hupei Province. (*Excavated* 1955.)

The Neolithic pottery of Hupei Province resembles neither typical Yang-shao coarse ware nor typical Lung Shan ware, but has traits related to both. Thus the goblet in Pl. 18b has the smooth black surface and angular profile typical of Lung Shan. The strange jug with three-lobed body called *k'uei* (Pl. 21) is also a type found in east and north-east China and characteristic of the black-pottery Neolithic culture. The *ting* (Pl. 20), on the other hand, is not found in the east coastal provinces or the north-east, but is common on Yang-shao sites in the Central Plain. The coarse red vase of Pl. 19b has a variety of impressed decoration which is increasingly abundant on Neolithic pottery as one moves from Honan eastwards, or southwards through the coastal provinces. Its shape, however, like that of the vessel shown in Pl. 19a, seems to be peculiar to Hupei.

The stone knife (Pl. 17a), a distinctive feature of Far Eastern Neolithic cultures in general, is found at Shih Chia Ho in the variety with curved back which is found chiefly in north China, especially on the lower course of the Yellow River and in the north-east. The stone axe (Pl. 17b) is of a form which survives into the Bronze Age, when it was also made in jade as a ritual instrument.

The bowl (Pl. 18a) features the only known example from a Neolithic site of the *t'ao t'ieh* monster-mask which is a common decorative motif on later bronze vessels. Its appearance here may indicate that the site is near in date to the Shang Bronze Age, or even contemporary with it.

Ref.: *K'ao Ku T'ung Hsün*, 56.3.11

PLATES 22–26 Hua T'ing Ts'un, Hsin I Hsien, Kiangsu Province. (*Excavated* 1953.)

The pottery found on Neolithic sites in Kiangsu Province displays a large variety of forms, some of which are related to those of the Central Plain, or to the types of the north-west Lung Shan tradition, while others have an individuality which sets them apart from both of these groups. The individual shapes are elaborate, sometimes with hard profiles and slender feet and handles somewhat alien to ceramic invention and suggesting metal prototypes. But no similar shapes are recorded in bronze.

The illustrated objects come from graves excavated at a Neolithic village site. The stone axes (Pl. 25) are typical of those found in east-central China. The surface of the pottery vessels is gritty, reddish and unburnished. The shapes of the jugs (Pls. 23, 26) and the *ting* are unparalleled.

Other objects recovered from the graves were stone bracelets and beads of a kind associated with the Neolithic of south-east China.

Ref.: *Wen Wu Ts'an K'ao Tzŭ Liao*, 1954.1.93; 1956.7.23.

PLATES 27–31 Liang Chu, Hang Hsien, Chekiang Province. (*Excavated* 1955.)

The black, burnished pottery recovered at this site closely resembles the finest ware from Ch'eng Tzŭ Yai, the type site of the Lung Shan culture in Shantung Province. The shapes have some individuality, suggesting a regional variation, but the angular outlines and clean, wheel-turned finish are quite similar. Even at Ch'eng Tzŭ Yai some of the ceramic forms hint at the possibility of related bronze shapes, although no metal was discovered on the site. Here the parallels to the shapes of Shang bronze vessels are more striking. The cup of Pl. 29a is close to the earliest form of *ku* as found at Hui Hsien (Pl. 44). The vessel shown in Pl. 29b is a *p'an*, the water-basin of the ritual bronzes, and the bowl of Pl. 31 is somewhat like the *yü* or *kuei* of the Shang and early Chou periods (*cf.* Pl. 63a). On the other hand the fruit-stand shape seen in Pl. 28, the *tou*, does not occur in bronze to join the ritual vessels until about half way through the Chou period, in the 6th century.

Liang Chu is the southernmost site on which Lung Shan pottery of such a pure strain has been recovered. In this region the traits of Lung Shan culture are usually found mingling with elements belonging to the south-east Neolithic.

PLATE 32 T'an Shih Shan, Min Hou Hsien, Fukien Province. (*Excavated* 1954.)

The Neolithic sites of the south-east and south coastal region, which are provisionally classed together as a South-east Neolithic province, often show a mixture of techniques in their pottery which suggests a crossing of cultural traditions no less complex than that found in the north. Since the chronology of the sites is still obscure it is possible that this impression is partly caused by the telescoping of influences which in reality were successive and more distinct than appears at present. The penetration of influences related to the Black Pottery Culture of the north-east can be traced as far south as Chekiang Province (*cf.* Hua T'ing Ts'un, Pls. 22–26, and Liang Chu, Pls. 27–31). In Fukien Province the pottery that predominates is decorated with geometric patterns impressed with wooden stamps, and this is combined, especially in Kuangtung Province, with a thin pottery, almost of stoneware hardness, impressed with more elaborate repetitive designs, the most striking of which has been called the 'double-f pattern'. The coarser ware sometimes includes a tripod vessel, but simple round-bottomed or ring-footed shapes are the rule. In the transitional region of Kiangsu and Chekiang the proportion of the coarse-stamped ware varies from place to place, but increases on the whole from north to south. It is in this region that individual assemblages of wares and shapes are chiefly found, such as those seen at Hua T'ing Ts'un and Liang Chu. In Fukien and Kuangtung the proportion of the finer, harder stamped ware increases further, and its manufacture probably persisted until late in the Bronze Age.

Throughout the coastal region, from Kiangsu southwards, the indications of economic life are fairly uniform. The sites are located for the most part on low hills or mounds or on the lower terraces of valley sides, and they are usually associated with great heaps of mollusc shells and some bones of wild animals, which suggests that fishing and hunting were more important sources of food than crops or cattle. The low-lying, well watered country to which this economy responded extends intermittently along the valleys of the Yangtze and its tributaries. The lake region surrounding the juncture of Anhui, Hupeh, Hunan and Kiangsi Provinces contains signs of similar settlements, sometimes marked by pottery of South-east Neolithic type, though occasionally, as at Shih Chia Ho, possessing a more individual character.

The site of T'an Shih Shan is on a low hog's back about 500 metres long, 10.4 metres wide and 10–20 metres above the present ground level, lying near the north bank of the Min river. Abundant mollusc shells (surprisingly, of salt-water species) and deers' antlers indicate a main source of food. The practice of agriculture is inferred rather doubtfully from the polished stone 'axes', the larger of which are interpreted as hoes, and from spindle-whorls, the sign of weaving, which is recognized as the all but universal concomitant of farming economy.

The stone axes and arrowheads are of the types commonly found on sites of the South-east Neolithic, with the exception of the second from the left in the top row. This piece (Pl. 32a) with its large central hole (*cf.* Shih Chia Ho, Pl. 17b) was probably used as a hoe in tillage; it is significantly absent from the south-east region as a whole, and commoner in the east and north. The pottery fragment (Pl. 32a, No. 6) is one of the rare examples from the site of the superior kind of ware with impressed decoration. No. 2 is the leg of a tripod vessel. This piece, together with Nos. 3–5 and 7, is decorated with black painted lines. These are the first examples of painted ware so far observed on a site of this type. It must reflect a remote influence from the Yang-shao culture of the Central Plain.

Ref.: *K'ao Ku Hsüeh Pao* 10.53.

PLATES 34–40 Erh Li Kang, Cheng Chou, Honan Province. (*Excavated* 1952.)

In recent years many sites of Neolithic and Shang dynasty date have been excavated near the town of Cheng Chou, in the east of Honan Province. The Bronze-Age levels in the excavations lay over Neolithic remains of both the Yang-shao and the Lung Shan traditions. Occupation was continuous from Neolithic times. Although tombs and building foundations were found scattered over an area of more than 25 square kilometres, it is clear that the whole of this space was not closely inhabited. The Bronze-Age habitations, like those of the Neolithic, were probably confined to pieces of ground raised slightly above the general level of the plain, and so less exposed to flooding from the Yellow River. Erh Li Kang itself is a low hog's back about a mile long and one-third of a mile wide. About a mile north of Erh Li Kang, near the excavated site of Tzŭ Ching Shan, the foundations of a city wall built of stamped earth, some 20 metres wide, were traced over a distance of more than a mile. At Tzŭ Ching Shan were discovered factories for bronze-founding and bone-working. At Ming Kung Lu a potter's establishment was identified. This evidence of massive fortification, and specialized industry, and the abundance of tools, weapons and pottery vessels unearthed from graves, house foundations and storage pits, indicate a centre probably even more populous than the Shang capital at Anyang, a hundred miles to the north. At Cheng Chou no remains have been found like those at Anyang which show this city to have been the seat of Shang kings – grandiose tombs, the foundations of large buildings and archives of stored oracle-bones with inscriptions – but phases of development indicated by pottery and other objects offer a means of dating sites within the Shang period such as were lacking previously. The Shang city at Cheng Chou, near the Yellow River in the heart of the Central Plain, was better placed strategically than Anyang for the political control of North China.

In the chronological succession suggested for the remains at Cheng Chou the lower level at Erh Li Kang is the second earliest, followed by the upper level at the same site and next by the material excavated at a site in the People's Park (Jen Min Kung Yüan). The earliest remains at Anyang are believed to reach no further back than the beginning of the latest phase at Cheng Chou, while the later phase at Anyang (that of the Royal Tombs) continues after it. This would indicate a date for the latest material so far excavated at Cheng Chou in the 15th or 14th century B.C. Sites at Cheng Chou corresponding to the age of the Shang kings recorded in the oracle-bone inscriptions still await discovery – they may be under the modern city.

Among the pieces illustrated the *li* with decoration of circles at the neck (Pl. 34), the trumpet-shaped vase (Pl. 39) and the *ting* (Pl. 35a) are characteristic of the upper level at Erh Li Kang. The decoration of the *ting* suggests the influence of the bronze versions of the same vessel. Later levels show gradual modifications of these shapes. The goblet of Plate 40 is an unusual Shang form. Pl. 38 shows one of the rare finds of ivory made on a Shang site, a goblet having the same unexplained cross-shaped perforation on the foot as appears among the bronze ritual vessels (*ku*).

An interesting development may be observed in the oracle bones. Their treatment is essentially the same as that found at Anyang: shallow pits are made in the bone and a hot bronze point is applied near them, the prognostication being made from the shape of the cracks which result. But whereas at Erh Li Kang the pits are single and round, those from the site in the People's Park are double, an oval pit overlapping each round one, which was the regular practice at Anyang. The Erh Li Kang bones are shoulder blades of ox, sheep and pig. At the People's Park carapaces of tortoise were also used, as at the capital. The only bone with an inscription recording the oracular question was found at Erh Li Kang.

Ref.: *K'ao Ku Hsüeh Pao*, 8.65; 1957.1.53.

PLATES 41–44 Liu Li Ko, near Hui Hsien, Honan Province (*Excavated* 1950.)

The many tombs excavated in the vicinity of the town of Hui Hsien range in date from the Shang to the Han dynasties (see Pl. 80–84). Over fifty near the village of Liu Li Ko all belong to the former. They were comparatively shallow rectangular pits dug in earth without reinforcement, some having the stepped side (*cf.* Pl. 45) and small pit beneath the body for the sacrificial dog, which follow the Shang custom, and all were furnished with pottery or bronze vessels. The site of houses was marked by deep storage pits. The Shang material recovered can be dated approximately by comparing the bronze vessels with those found at Cheng Chou (Pls. 34–40) and Anyang. Their style is close to that of vessels from the former place, and is paralleled by only a small number of pieces belonging to the earlier phase of the capital. Their date may therefore be in the 15th or 14th century B.C. They have primitive features in shape and ornament. The angular profile and flat bottom of the *chüeh* (Pl. 43) and the profile of the *chia* (Pl. 42) are characteristic of the earliest forms. The *li* (Pl. 41) is closer in shape to the pottery vessel from which it derives (*cf.* Pl. 35a) than are the corresponding late Shang vessels of Anyang. The squatter shape of the *ku* (Pl. 44) compares poorly with the evolved form (Pl. 52), although it is already characteristic in the disposal of the ornament and the presence of the cruciform hole of unknown purpose (*cf.* Pl. 38). On the other hand the ornament is evolved far beyond the more or less realistic animal mask – the *t'ao t'ieh* or 'glutton mask' – from which it seems to have originated. A Neolithic example of the motif suggests its simpler ancestor (*cf.* Pl. 18a). Here the mask itself and its lateral extensions (often described as the body of the *t'ao t'ieh*) are freely treated as linear pattern. The eyes, as always, remain prominent. The rendering of the ornament falls short of the finer Shang work, although it already indicates a considerable mastery of bronze casting.

The *li* and the *chia* were found in the same tomb, and the *chüeh* and *ku* in another. The second combination is the commonest among the grave deposits of bronze vessels in Shang times.

Ref.: *Report on the Hui Hsien Excavations*, 1956.

PLATES 45–52 Ta Ssŭ K'ung Ts'un, Anyang, Honan Province. (*Excavated* 1953.)

The great tombs of Anyang, believed to be the burials of Shang kings, are situated at distances of a few miles from the city of Great Shang. Near the village of Ta Ssŭ Kung was discovered a group of graves of comparable importance, though one of royal size was not traced. The graves were mostly of the type shown complete with its furniture of pottery and bronzes in Pl. 45. The bodies were regularly laid prone. The greatest interest attaches to the burial of a chariot with charioteer and horses (Pl. 46) which careful excavation laid bare in quite undisturbed condition. Such chariot burials had been discovered previously at Anyang, as the accompaniment of a royal funeral or of the holocaust performed in an inauguration ceremony. In the present pit earth traces recorded the positions and shape of the vanished wood of wheels, axle and main beam, and the foundation of the driver's box. The traces are marked by lines of bronze discs which decorated them. Over each horse's neck lay the bronze sheathing of a wooden yoke (Pl. 47) on which the weight of the shaft rested. The bronze axle-caps are seen still in place. In and near the box are strewn bronzes: arrowheads, a knife and two bow-shaped objects (Pl. 48). The purpose of these last remains unexplained; they cannot, from their shape, be ornaments for bows, as was long believed, and it is difficult to see how they could have been firmly enough attached to serve as rein-guides or grips on the chariot box. They may have been mounted on shields, now perished. In another chariot pit which contained the bodies of two charioteers, they also occurred as a pair. The knife is of the 'Siberian' type regularly found in the chariot burials. The type of ornament seen on the harness mounts (Pl. 49) is characteristic of chariot bronzes, and somewhat distinct in character from the typical Shang decoration of the sacrificial bronze vessels. It is more akin to the style found on bronze vessels of the early Chou period.

It is not yet certain whether the method of harnessing chariot horses was like that of the ancient Near East, Greece and Rome, in which the animals pulled on a broad band passed around the neck, or already approximated to that known in China from the 1st century B.C., in which the strain was taken more effectively by the horse's chest and shoulders. The fact that two horses are required here to pull a relatively light chariot, and that another similar chariot burial contained four horses, suggests that the less efficient method was in use in China also in this early period.

The wine bucket, *yu* (Pl. 50), takes the form of an animal, presumably two addorsed owls, such as survives complete with lid in some specimens of better workmanship. Owls are believed to have figured among the sacrificial animals of Shang. The *ku* goblet is of the finest quality, in elegance of shape as much as in the delicate rendering of the ornament. This is based on a 'dissolved' version of the dominant *t'ao t'ieh* motif, the lines of the mask forming separated units set around two unmistakable eyes. In the middle section a conventional dragon motif is similarly dismembered. Immediately above are two serpentine creatures called silkworms by antiquarians. The beautiful lanceolate ornaments rising to the lip have features reminiscent of the stylized treatment of dragon motifs.

Ref.: *K'ao Ku Hsüeh Pao*, 9.25.

PLATES 54–55 Wu Kuan Ts'un, Anyang, Honan Province. (*Excavated* 1950.)

Excavation of the deep tomb at Wu Kuan Ts'un near Anyang has given us the clearest picture of the features of a 'royal' Shang tomb. Others of equal size have been investigated, but were found to have been badly damaged by grave-robbers, or could not be satisfactorily published owing to the troubles of the war. At Wu Kuan Ts'un too robbers had succeeded in reaching the central burial chamber to remove the more valuable contents. The excavations carried out in 1950, however, revealed the ceremonial burials which accompanied the principal entombment still undisturbed. The photograph shows clearly the rectangular main chamber. It originally contained inner and outer coffins built of massive timbers. Beneath is a small pit – the so-called 'waist-pit' – for the foundation sacrifice of a dog, whose skeleton has frequently survived in other graves. The top of the outer coffin would reach approximately to the level of the broad step on which the bodies of the sacrificed persons were laid. The great tombs are either cruciform in plan, having a long ramp rising gradually to the ground surface from each side, or elongated, with only two ramps, as in the present example. Here, as in at least one other tomb, the northern ramp is interrupted by pits containing the skeletons of many horses, and probably (though at Wu Kuan Ts'un this was not established) the burial of a chariot. In both tombs the northern ramp ends in steps at the lower end. These tombs were levelled on the surface and are now sometimes traceable by depressions formed over them. The custom of raising barrows over important tombs seems not to have been introduced until Han times.

The only worked object found in the tomb was the *ch'ing*, or musical stone (Pl. 55) which can be seen lying *in situ* on the pit shelf. The conventionalized tiger which decorates it is depicted in rounded raised line from which the background has been rubbed down. Sounding stones were to become a regular feature of Chinese ceremonial music. They existed in the Chou period in sets answering to the notes of a musical scale.

Ref.: *K'ao Ku Hsüeh Pao*, 5.1.

PLATES 57–62 Hai Tao Ying Tzŭ Ts'un, Ling Yüan Hsien, Jehol Province. (*Discovered in* 1955.)

A farmer discovered this group of bronze vessels while ploughing on a hill slope where they lay under a shallow covering of soil. There was no sign of a tomb. Potsherds, fragments of stone axes and sickles and ash-stained earth were noted in the vicinity. No excavation has yet taken place to ascertain how this rather disparate collection of vessels came to be preserved at this spot. A number of them have been repaired in ancient times, and some are blackened with soot from ancient use. This is only the second recorded find of bronze vessels in Jehol Province, which lay on the edge of the territory ruled by Shang and by the central Chou state of the Chou confederacy.

The forms and decoration of the bronzes are distinct in some respects from similar vessels found further west. If they are assumed to have been manufactured in the space of a generation or two, some features may indicate a mixture of traditions, or a provincial backwardness. Thus one bowl, a handle-less *kuei* with whirligig discs in the neck and sides covered with nipples, is quite in the Shang manner. The form of the handled bowl, a *yü* (Pl. 61), is peculiar to North Honan and the late Shang period, but the decoration which appears on it belongs to the art of the early Chou period, and seems to be not earlier than 1000 B.C. The *hsien* (Pl. 58), a steamer divided by a grating at the centre, is of a type which begins in Shang, and survives until about 900 B.C. in the Chou period. The *kuei* of Pl. 60 is not a normal Shang type, although one like it has been excavated at Anyang. It is present in groups of vessels excavated near Loyang, in central Honan, and is perhaps a form of Chou rather than Shang tradition. But here the animal mask set between remnants of a dissolved *t'ao t'ieh* is quite unlike any ornament known on vessels found in any part of Honan. The *ting* (Pl. 62) is unparalleled in shape, but the procession of birds in the ornamental band is characteristic of vessels of the 10th century B.C.

The *kuei* (Pl. 60) is inscribed with a single character *ts'ai*, which is probably the name of the person for whom it was made. The *yu* (Pl. 57) has the inscription 'The scribe Fa had made this sacrificial vessel (for sacrifice to) his ancestor Jen (*cf.* introduction, p. 13), and the *yü* (Pl. 61) was 'Made by the Marquis of Yen'.

Ref.: *Wen Wu Ts'an K'ao Tzŭ Liao*, 1955.8.16.

PLATES 63–66 Yen Tun Shan, Tan T'u Hsien, Kiangsu Province. (*Excavated in* 1954.)

Like the preceding group, these vessels were a

chance find made by a farmer on the slope of a hill overlooking the Yangtze River. They lay together in a shallow pit presumed to be a grave. What was said of the provincial appearance of the preceding group of bronzes as compared with the better known vessels of Honan and Shansi applies here also, but with one exception. This is the *kuei* (Pl. 63b). Its shape, with four massive handles capped by animal heads, and the rendering of the ornament in a rounded line raised on a plain background, is reminiscent of the famous Hsing Hou *kuei* in the British Museum. The hooked flanges on the foot also are typical of the earliest style of vessels cast under the Chou dynasty, in the late 11th and early 10th centuries B.C. The decoration in the band around the foot is a variety of pacing dragon. On the sides there are dragons with heads reverted and jaws agape. The figure over the head of each is recognizable in other examples of this pattern as a little snake resembling the 'silk-worm' on the *ku* of Pl. 52. But the main interest of this vessel is the inscription cast on it. It records a sacrifice made by the second Chou king, Ch'eng, to his father Wu Wang, who had led the attack on the Shang kingdom; Ch'eng Wang has 'subjugated the Shang' i.e. the rebellion of the Shang which had taken place after their defeat, and 'visited the eastern region'. He grants a fief in Yi to one Nieh. From mentions of this person on other bronze vessels it is inferred that he was first with Ch'eng Wang at the Chou capital near Loyang in Honan; and then accompanied him on the campaign to Shantung and the east coast which confirmed Chou control of that region. The whereabouts of Yi where Nieh is now installed as feudal ruler is not known – it may be in Kiangsu, in the district where the group of bronzes was found.

The bronzes form a complete set or perhaps two sets of vessels for use in the ceremony of prayer and sacrifice. They are as follows:

For preparing food:	1 *li* 1 *ting*
For holding food:	2 *kuei* (Pls. 63a, b)
For warming wine:	2 *ho* (Pl. 66)
For holding wine:	2 *kuang* (Pl. 65)
For libation	2 *chiao* (Pl. 64a)
Water-vessels	2 *p'an* (Pl. 64b)

The libation goblets copy the shape of horns (*chiao*), and are unique, the normal form being the tripod goblets called *chüeh*. But by the absence of the *chüeh* and of the *ku* goblet this set of vessels differs from those typical of the Shang and early Chou period in Honan. The shapes of the *kuang* and *ho* and the ornament on the sides of the *p'an* and the *kuei* of Pl. 63a are also distinct from the contemporary bronzes from central China, and must represent a local variation. It seems to follow from the inscription that the *kuei* was cast either during Ch'eng Wang's lifetime, or at latest just after his death, in the reign of K'ang Wang, i.e. at the end of the 11th or the beginning of the 10th century B.C.

The historian Ch'en Meng-chia draws a number of important conclusions from the inscription: (*a*) that the territory of Yi is in the district where the find was made (on the assumption that the bronzes came from a grave) and that the Chou had already extended their political control to the coastal region; (*b*) that the historical record of Ch'eng Wang's campaign to the east is corroborated, the king being free to act, and not under the tutelage of the Duke of Chou as has been transmitted; (*c*) the king being still alive at the time when the inscription was composed, Ch'eng is his actual and not his posthumous name.

Ref.: *Wen Wu Ts'an K'ao Tzŭ Liao*, 1955.5.58.

PLATES 67–69 P'u Tu Ts'un, Ch'ang an Hsien, Shensi Province. (*Excavated in* 1954.)

Attention was drawn to this site when a villager dug out the wine vessel (Pl. 69) from the yard of his house. Excavation revealed a rectangular pit grave of the early type, 4.2 metres long, 2.25 metres wide, and 3.6 metres deep, with stepped side and foundation pit containing the skeleton of a dog. The grave contained three human skeletons, and 15 bronze and 16 pottery vessels, the latter heaped together in a corner. Finds of bronzes in Shensi are rare. Apart from the fine quality of the wine vessels this group holds great interest for its location – which is about 40 kms. west of the site of Hao, a capital of the Chou dynasts before and for some time after their conquest of the Shang –

and for the inscription cast on the wine ewer. The latter was made to commemorate an honour conferred on its owner by the Chou king Mu, who ruled for about 20 years in the middle of the 10th century B.C.

The form of the handle of the wine ewer, with its decoration of an animal head something like a deer (*cf.* Pl. 60), follows a convention which was introduced in central China at the time of the Chou conquest. The ornamental bands on the neck and lid are composed of units of linear pattern disposed around a central 'eye', suggesting a derivation from an animal motif, related to the dragons of Shang in earlier centuries. On the wine-vessel (Pl. 68) the pattern is purely formal, with no apparent relation to the conventional animal designs.

The bell (Pl. 67) is one of the earliest examples of this type dated by the evidence of inscription, and the earliest unearthed in a controlled excavation. Series of such bells were used in ceremonial music: a set giving a scale of 13 notes has been discovered, complete with its lacquered wooden stand, at Hsin Yang in Honan Province. These bells are of the 5th or 4th century B.C., but their shape is very similar to those of early Chou date.

Ref.: *K'ao Ku Hsüeh Pao*, 1957.1.75.

PLATES 70–77 Shou Hsien, Anhwei Province. (*Excavated* 1955.)

Shou Hsien is in the territory of the ancient state of Wu, where a Marquis of Chao of the neighbouring state of Ts'ai took refuge in 493 B.C. after an army of the southern Ch'u kingdom had overrun his domains. Ts'ai was finally destroyed in 447 B.C. The name of the Marquis of Ts'ai inscribed on some of the 486 vessels, weapons, chariot-mounts and ornamental bronzes recovered from this tomb is written with an ideograph which cannot be identified with any member of the Ts'ai house recorded in history. Nevertheless the tomb dates probably from the period of exile of the Ts'ai rulers in Wu, between 493 and 447 B.C.

When about thirty years ago another tomb in the vicinity of Shou Hsien was exploited by antique dealers the flood of bronzes which reached museums and collectors led to the recognition of a distinct style of bronze art belonging to this region of China, the Huai river basin. The Huai style, as Karlgren named it, is seen here in its most developed form. It represents a climax of trends apparent in the development of the bronze ornament a century earlier in central China, although there it did not achieve such elaboration. Its essential feature is a continuous pattern of small curving units which have been called 'spiral and feather' or 'teeming hooks'. The linear basis of the design has been so reduced in scale that it appears as a lively rippling of the surface (*cf.* Pl. 70) or sometimes as a mere granulation. Its effect, in the outstanding examples of the work, depends even more than that of the older ornament on flawless rendering in the casting. In the present group of vessels the casting is not of the finest quality.

The bronzes illustrated here show some of the forms assumed by the ceremonial vessels in the 5th century B.C. The old categories have been abandoned; the stranger shapes of the Shang and early Chou vessels no longer appear. The *ting* (Pl. 77), which persisted until Han times has the inelegant profile which was now peculiar to the south-east provinces, and was the form produced in the southern state of Ch'u now that its kings imitated the Chou rulers by casting bronze vessels of their own. The *kuei* (Pl. 75) is more faithful in shape to the early style, but the ornament on the lid is an innovation. The water bowl called *chien* (Pl. 73) and the food-vessel called *tui* (Pl. 74) are shapes which now appear for the first time.

The tiger-handles and animal feet of the tall wine jar (Pl. 71) show the advent of a new kind of stylized animal art. The bells recovered from the tomb include a set of twelve of graded size which lay together. The *chien* is exceptional in being inscribed 'Chien of King Kuang of Wu'. It is surmised that it reached the Ts'ai household as a gift, possibly in the dowry of a daughter of the king who married into the Ts'ai family.

Ref.: *Objects Recovered from the Tomb of the Marquis of Ts'ai at Shou Hsien*, 1956.

PLATE 78 Hsing Lung Hsien, Jehol Province. (*Excavated* 1955.)

Whereas in the west iron-casting was not known until the middle ages, in China it was practised from the first introduction of the metal, probably about 600 B.C. It was possible to mould more elaborate shapes than could be produced under the hammer. In the late Chou period iron gradually displaced bronze as the metal for tools, although for weapons it was not generally adopted until the middle of the 3rd century B.C. Even after the discovery of iron, bronze might be used for commonplace tools. This mould is intended for casting 'socketed' axes in bronze. This bag-shaped axe or adze was in use in China from the Shang period onwards, having reached China from the far west about the 13th or 12th century B.C. Various shapes of the socketed axe are common in the north, in the region of the Great Wall, and can be most closely matched in late Bronze-Age sites in the Minusinsk area of South Siberia.

PLATES 79–84 Liu Li Ko, Chao Ku and Ku Wei Ts'un, Hui Hsien, Honan Province. (*Excavated* 1950.)

Besides the tombs of Shang date (*v.* Pls. 41–44), some undisturbed tombs of the 4th–3rd century B.C. were excavated near the town of Hui Hsien. At Liu Li Ko the most surprising discovery was the burial of nineteen chariots in a pit measuring 7.8 metres by 21 metres, and 4.4 metres deep. The chariots had been arranged in two rows, the shaft of each resting on the box of the one in front. The bronze parts (principally axle-caps and pieces mounted on the harnessing yoke, on the ends of shafts and posts of the hand-rails) had nearly all been removed before the chariots were buried. In nearly every case the shapes of the timbers of shaft, wheels and box were recoverable almost in their entirety from traces left in the earth by the now wholly vanished wood. Some of the hand-rails and box sides were covered with lacquer paint, which being imperishable, marked their position very clearly. Elsewhere only soil colour and texture distinguished the earth filling of the pit from the fine, compact soil which had taken the place of the wood as it rotted away. With consummate excavator's skill Mr Hsia Nai, the Deputy Director of the Institute of Archaeology, performed the feat of recovering a 'ghost' from the soil, such as was witnessed in England in 1939 in the excavation of the Sutton Hoo Ship-burial.

Plate 79 shows the excavation as completed. The figure below shows one form of chariot as reconstructed by the excavators. Another form differed slightly in dimensions and in having the wheels 'dished', i.e. the rim advanced outwards beyond the plane in which the spokes enter the hub, and was strengthened by two parallel straight struts crossing near the diameter. The chariots had presumably been part of a funeral procession. The horses which had drawn them were slaughtered and buried in an annexe at one end of the chariot pit; but unlike the practice of Shang times, the charioteers were spared. No human burial corresponding to the chariot pit could be found, though local memories recalled the discovery nearby of a tomb with bronze vessels before the late war. The indications of yokes and shafts suggest that the method of harnessing had not progressed beyond that of Shang times (p. 22). Two horses were still required to pull a small, light chariot.

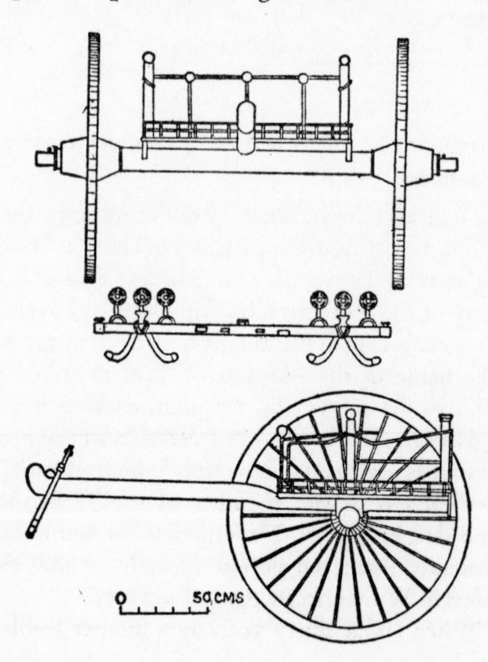

Some 10 kilometres to the south-west of Hui Hsien, near the village of Chao Ku, a few late Chou graves were excavated, of which one contained over 150 items of bronze – vessels, weapons and harness parts. Among the vessels was the *hu* of Pl. 80 and the *hsien* of Pl. 81. Near Ku Wei Ts'un, close to Hui Hsien, six late Chou tombs were investigated, of which three consisted of elaborately constructed wooden chambers at the bottom of pits measuring up to ten metres square in the lowest part, and 18 metres deep. One had long approach-ramps to north and south in the tradition which survived since Shang times.

The jade pendant illustrated in Pl. 82b came from one of these large tombs, where it lay with other jade objects in a separate cache. The jade is white with a slight green tinge. The five central parts are hollow and held together by a bronze band passing through them which ends in animal masks of gilded bronze holding the terminal pieces in their jaws. The style of the animal heads and of the interlacery pattern covering the three middle sections is similar to that found in bronze ornament of the 4th century B.C. The glass beads of Pl. 82a come from the same tomb.

The belt-hook of Pl. 83a is of silver, gilded on the upper surface. The ornament, in sharp-edged relief, consists of tiger and dragon masks at the ends and two griffin-like animals at the sides. Of the three inlaid jade rings the two outer still enclose variegated glass beads; the bead of the middle ring is missing. The jade pendant and this belt-hook are two of the most splendid ornaments which have survived from the pre-Han period, and the finest recovered in systematic excavations.

Ref.: *Report on the Hui Hsien Excavations*, 1956.

PLATES 85–88 Chia Ko Chuang, T'ang Shan Shih, Hopei Province.

In 1953, 42 graves were excavated near the mining town of T'ang Shan Shih. About one half of them proved to belong to the 5th–4th centuries B.C., and the remainder to the early Han period. Grave No. 18, which contained the bronze vessels in Pls. 85–87, was the largest of all, a rectangular pit with vertical walls, measuring 5 by 4.2 metres, and 1.44 metres deep. The buried vessels included also one each of the forms *p'an*, *kuei* and *ting*, besides weapons and harness and chariot bronzes. Unfortunately it was not possible to ascertain whether an entire chariot had been buried. The food vessel and *tui* (Pl. 88) and the wine vase called *hu* were found alongside in smaller graves.

The decoration of these vessels represents a hitherto unknown local variation of the bronze art of the later Chou period. The style seen in the pattern covering the body of the *tui*, and the scale and plait patterns of the *yi*, is intermediate between that of the important group of bronzes discovered in 1923 at Li Yü Ts'un in Shansi Province and the Huai style typified by the finds at Shou Hsien (Pls. 70–77). The conventional treatment of animal shapes is closer to the latter. It has a number of features strongly reminiscent of the animal art of the Asiatic steppes, particularly the spirals placed over the joints of limbs, and the spirals and comma-shaped figures on snouts, jaws and ears. What historical connexion there may be – whether China was the recipient or originator of this trend in graphic art – remains uncertain, although the relationship cannot be doubted.

The decoration of the wine jar (Pl. 86) consists of hunting scenes cast in shallow but clear relief and inlaid with a black substance. Here also spiralized figures appear on the animals' bodies. Wild boar, deer and birds look like real game, but a phoenix is fanciful, and the elephant-like creature problematic, since elephants have not existed wild in Central China in historical times. The huntsmen have spears and one is accompanied by a dog. A number of such wine vases with this type of decoration are preserved in collections, but the present example is the first that has been found in a supervised excavation and associated in a group with other vessels. One 'hunting *hu*' has an inscription recording a sacrifice at a place in Hopei Province; and a *yi* mentions a prince of Yen. It seems clear that all these vessels were made in the state of Yen and reflect a style which was rooted there. Yen preserved its identity from the 8th century B.C. until its extinction by Ch'in in the unification of 232 B.C. Its territory embraced the two north-eastern provinces of Liao Ning and Hopei, and the northern part of the Korean peninsula, and was in easy contact with the nomadic tribes living farther north. An influence of the animal art of the steppes may have passed more easily from north to south in the east-coast region of China than it could across the central plain, to the north and north-west of which lay more difficult country.

The shapes of the vessels are broadly speaking those found in other parts of China at this period. *Tui*, *tou*, and 'hunting *hu*' are all new forms of vessels, probably as much used on ordinary occasions as in ceremonial and sacrifice. They appear about 500 B.C.

The date of the T'ang Shan vessels is probably in the early 5th century B.C., rather earlier than those from Shou Hsien. In the representation of animals there are points of comparison with the two inscribed *hu* in the Cull collection in London, which are dated through an historical allusion to the year 482 B.C.

Ref.: *K'ao Ku Hsüeh Pao*, 6.57.

PLATES 89–97 Ch'ang Sha, Hunan Province. (*Excavated* 1953–4.)

Outside the walls of Ch'ang Sha, the chief town of Hunan Province, many tombs of the 3rd–1st centuries B.C. have been discovered in recent years in the course of public works. They often contained wooden and lacquered objects remarkably well preserved through the dampness of the sandy soil in which the tombs were dug. The latter are formed of rectangular boxes built of massive timbers, measuring as much as 5 by 4 metres in area, and 2–3 metres in depth, lying at the bottom of a vertical pit 3 to 8 metres deep. These are the outer coffins, in which inner coffins, also of wood, were neatly fitted. Ch'ang Sha was the site of the capital of the southern state of Ch'u whose attacks on its northern neighbours were the chief cause of disturbance in central China before the eastward expansion of Ch'in which led to the unification. Even during the troubles of the 'Age of the Warring States', Ch'ang Sha was comparatively peaceful. In Han times the district was at one time placed under the rule of local kings. The tombs of the third century usually contain weapons in addition to pottery and bronze vessels. From the beginning of the Han period, in 206 B.C., weapons are no longer found among the grave goods.

Some of the objects buried with the dead reflect superstitious beliefs apparently distinct from those of other parts of China. Such, for example, is a wooden carving of a human head with a long protruding tongue and crowned with deer antlers, now in the British Museum. The figures in Pl. 97 are carved in the same rough style. Retinues of such servants, originally painted in black and red and some of them having movable arms, were buried for the convenience of their dead master. The tombs contained tables, musical instruments, toilet boxes, cups and other objects of lacquered wood, decorated with designs in red and yellow on a black ground. The toilet boxes preserved their contents of wooden combs and hairpins, bronze mirrors, beads (Pls. 89a 90, 94). The wine cups (Pls. 91, 93) are of the usual Han shape. They were placed on stands consisting of two parallel bars, on which the side flanges of the cups rested.

The patterns which decorate the lacquered objects are inherited from the art of the late Chou period represented by the bronze ornament. In the Han period they were copied and modified in the official factories which produced lacquered articles for government use and bestowal. Some of the factories were situated in Szechwan Province, where the lacquer tree grew in abundance. The 'Western Factory of Shu Commandery' produced cups and bowls of which examples survive with inscribed dates ranging from 85 B.C. to A.D. 71. Some of the inscriptions name no fewer than 13 individuals, from painters and polishers to the corporal of the factory guard, who were concerned with the work.

The writing brush (Pl. 89b) is the earliest which has survived.

Ref.: *Report on the Ch'ang Sha Excavations*, 1957.

PLATES 98–105 Wang Tu Hsien, Hopei Province. (*Excavated* 1954.)

In the first century A.D. the old log-built tombs were superseded by subterranean vaults, which in the more grandiose examples comprised several chambers with connecting passages. The largest and best preserved brick tomb excavated so far is one situated about a mile east of the town of Wang Tu, though in size and complexity it is followed closely by others of similar type recently excavated in the suburbs of Canton. The brick-built tombs make use of barrel-vaulting and true arches. At Wang Tu there are three main chambers orientated north-south, with five smaller side chambers, the whole with the entrance passage measuring over 20 metres in length. The roofs over the main chambers are double vaulted. A number of such tombs retain part of their mural decoration, but none other so completely as the tomb at Wang Tu.

The paintings are executed in yellow, blue and red, with heavy black outline. Most of them are preserved on the east and west walls of the southernmost chamber, the antechamber, (*cf.* Pl. 100). The upper frieze contains officials bowing northwards towards the occupants of the tomb. The second and fourth to the right of the doorway are illustrated in Pls. 104 and 101. Both hold the courtiers' *hu*, an oblong plaque used to cover the face. One is designated by inscription 'Meritorious official within the Gate', and the other 'Penal Officer within the Gate'. Both titles belong to government officers attached to the *chün* territorial administration, and the phrase 'within the gate' denotes a great household. The occupant of the grave must have been the governor of a *chün* or an officer of similar rank. An obviously young man on the east wall of the antechamber is a 'minor scribe' of the household (Pl. 102) and a group of men on the same wall (Pl. 103) is designated 'Eight men of the Fives and Hundreds of the Official Carriages'. This must refer to the staff of carriages and relays under command of the *chün* which was responsible in its territory for the postal system essential to the centralized administration of the Han emperors.

A further inscription records that all the officials 'eat from the Great Granary', i.e. are entitled to receive grain from the government store. The white hare of Pl. 105 belongs to the lower frieze of auspicious animals: in the moon he pounds the herbs of the elixir of life. Opposite, the painting of a cock is inscribed 'Marquis Cock even in the night breaks not faith'.

Ref.: *Murals of the Han Tomb at Wang Tu*, 1955.

PLATES 106–109 Hsin Tsao Hsiang, Mien Yang Hsien, Szechwan Province. (*Excavated* 1953.)

The Han tombs of Szechwan Province, mostly of the 1st and 2nd centuries A.D., are remarkably rich in sculpture and bas-reliefs. The pottery tableau of Pl. 106a shows a farmer or landowner with his family standing next to a pond which may represent a rice field. In it are models of lotus buds, frogs and water-snails. The musician of Pl. 106b is playing the *Sê* lute. Pl. 107 shows a dancer, one of the best portrayals in a statuette of a motif commonly found impressed or incised on bricks.

Cf. *K'ao Ku Hsüeh Pao*, 1958.1.57.

PLATES 110–114 Pei Chai Ts'un, I-nan, Shantung Province. (*Excavated* 1953–4.)

This subterranean tomb is built throughout of monolithic stone pillars and beams, conforming closely to the style of Chinese wooden architecture. Like the tomb at Wang Tu (Pls. 98–105) it consists of three main chambers extending north to south, with a south-facing entrance. The stone capitals imitate the wooden forms. During the following twelve hundred years the single boat-shaped bracket (Pl. 110a) was destined to be multiplied and elaborated as a crucial element, both structural and decorative, in the architecture of China, Korea and Japan. The corbelled vault raised over the principal bays (Pl. 114) anticipates the 'lantern roof' found in later wooden buildings.

But the greatest interest of the tomb lies in the bas-relief and engraved decoration which covers most of the surface of pillars and architraves. As a mythological document this tomb is comparable to the famous tomb of Wu Liang, also in Shantung Province, and also of the Later Han period. The taste for decoration drawn from myth and legend seems to have been particularly strong in Shantung

Province, which at this period was one of the most Confucian-minded and traditionalist parts of China. The stories and supernatural beliefs illustrated were, however, common to the whole area of Chinese civilization.

The architrave of the entrance represents a battle of foot-soldiers on a bridge (Pl. 110b). On the left cavalry advances over mountainous country; on the right, behind the infantry, is a typical Han carriage holding a personage wearing what appears to be the hat of civil officialdom. Beneath the bridge are soldiers fallen among fish and a boat with three oarsmen and two passengers. A similar scene is depicted at the Wu Liang tomb. The subject is more likely to be mythological than historical, though the story has not been identified.

The largest figure on the middle pillar of the entrance is a Feathered Man such as figures in most Taoist scenes portrayed in Han art. Above, a soldier is drawing his cross-bow, the bolt between his teeth. The human-faced quadruped which seems to be held aloft by the Feathered Man is winged and possibly horned. It is a flying animal of Taoist myth, but whether dragon, tiger or deer is uncertain. At the bottom of the panel is a monster mask with gaping mouth and large clawed feet.

The right-hand pillar of the entrance has at the top the figures of Fu Hsi (to the right with set-square) and his female partner Nü Wa (to the left with compasses). These two culture-heroes, conceived as half human, half serpent, had in Han times already been euhemerized as ancient historical emperors. The identity of the personage who appears between them is not clear. It may be the Yellow Emperor, who was sometimes placed at the head of the earliest rulers. Below is Hsi Wang Mu – 'Queen Mother of the West' – a Taoist deity who presided over a paradise of immortals in the West, and was paired with Tung Wang Kung – 'Lord King of the East'.

The tomb was built probably near the end of the Han period, about A.D. 200.

Ref.: *Report on the Excavation of the Stone Tomb with Figured Walls at Yi Nan*, 1956.

PLATES 115–117 Lung Sheng Kang, Canton, Kuangtung Province. (*Excavated* 1953.)

The tomb from which these objects were recovered was of the type which survived from Chou times into the early Han period. It consisted of a rectangular chamber, about 4 by 6 metres in plan, divided into three by partition walls. The first chamber, to which the entrance ramp led, was reserved for grave goods. The remainder of the chamber was divided longitudinally to receive two coffins, that on the left for a woman, apparently buried earlier than her husband, who occupied the right-hand space. The burials are believed to have taken place between A.D. 20 and A.D. 50. The grave deposits consisted of pottery vessels and pottery models of a house; a store-house raised on pillars; a well-head and a cooking stove; beads of cornelian, crystal and glass; a small carving of a lion in agate; a gold ornament in the form of an open-work polyhedron with granulation; some weapons and the fragmentary remains of many lacquered objects.

The plates illustrate some of these last. The plaques shown in Pl. 115 have projections at the side possibly meant for attaching them to the sides of a box. The dog-tooth and triangles-with-spirals of the border and the cloud scrolls of the main field are characteristic motifs of Han art. The crane in Pl. 115a was probably already associated with Taoism and symbolized longevity, as it has continued to do to the present time. The raging animal in Pl. 115b, who appears also adorning the shield shown in Pl. 116b, is Ch'ih Yu, a legendary being, half animal and half human, who personified military virtue and enjoyed a cult in the army. The Feathered Man drawn against scrollery in Pl. 116a is a creature of Taoist myth. Feathered Men are depicted also on bronze mirrors as attendants of Hsi Wang Mu (Queen Mother of the West) and Tung Wang Kung (Lord King of the East), the chief gods of the Taoists. On this lacquer their representative is given a monkey-like face such as does not appear elsewhere. Taoist deities and their trains were conceived to pass at will through the sky. Monkeys and tigers alike were denizens of the mountainous west where the paradise of Taoist immortals was imagined to be. Of this piece only the lacquer skin has survived, the wooden base having wholly perished.

Plate 117 shows three views of the wooden stock and mechanism of a cross-bow. In the middle picture may be seen the groove on which the end of the bolt lay. When the bowstring was drawn back it pressed against the projecting lever, whereupon two teeth rose through the slots on the plate to hold it. The mechanism became locked in this position by the action of a lever falling into place under its own weight (the weapon being pointed downwards). Pressure on the trigger then released the shot. The cross-bow became a regular weapon of the Chinese army in the 1st century B.C. Its possession undoubtedly made easier the defence of the Great Wall against nomad inroads, a task which consumed the greater part of the military resources of the Han emperors.

Ref.: *K'ao Ku Hsüeh Pao*, 1957.1.141.

PLATES 118, 119 Western Suburb of Loyang, Honan Province. (*Excavated* 1954.)

Han tombs have yielded pottery vessels, figurines and models, mirrors, vessels and ornaments of bronze in great abundance. But until excavations were begun at Loyang no habitation sites of the Han period had been investigated other than fortresses on the Great Wall. Pl. 119 shows a selection of everyday objects found in Han houses. Iron is now in general use. The knives at the top and centre are little different from some still used in North China. Between them is a sickle, and to the right of it a belt-hook – an object more usually made of bronze. The ring-handled knives differ only in size from the type of single-edged sword, made both in iron and bronze, which displaced the shorter two-edged variety towards the end of the 3rd century B.C., and probably formed the chief arm of the Ch'in armies in their conquest.

Pl. 118 shows a house floor. The wall footings are of compressed earth.

PLATES 120, 121 Eastern Suburb, Canton, Kuangtung Province. (*Excavated* 1955.)

The Later Han tomb which contained these models is an elaborate 'bee-hive' structure of brick with two main chambers connected by a low vaulted transept. The grave goods amounted to 249 items, including bronze mirrors, pottery incense burners and pottery models of halberds, spears, dancers and musicians, a horse and cart, and the boat and walled town-house shown here.

The boat (Pl. 121) is flat-bottomed, decked and provided with rudder-oar and tholes for three oars a side towards the prow. The deck-houses resemble those still to be seen on the Pearl River at Canton. They are roofed with matting and communicate below decks. There are six men aboard. The rudder-oar is mounted on the larboard side, in contrast to the starboard rudder of the west. A wooden model of a boat was found also in another Han tomb at Ch'ang-sha in Hunan. Like the model carriages which were sometimes buried it represents the conveyance of a rich citizen or important official.

The walled house (Pl. 120) has five compartments inside, set either side of the central court, and roofed with tiles. The front wall has the legend 'great good luck' inscribed on it.

Ref.: *K'ao Ku T'ung Hsün*, 1957.4.22.

PLATES 122, 123 Shih Chai Shan, Ning Hsien, Yunnan Province.

The small hill of Shih Chai, about 70 miles south of Kunming in a wild part of Yunnan, was probably once an island in the Tien Ch'ih lake, or lay nearer to its shore than it does at the present time. The place was occupied over a long period. The earliest inhabitants had accumulated a mound of shells of the freshwater molluscs which were an important source of food. Grain impressions on pottery fragments and spindle weights show that they were acquainted with agriculture and weaving. At another place on the hill an earth grave containing a body laid on its side with flexed legs, accompanied by a few pots, is similar to graves found in Kansu Province, and distinct from the Neolithic graves of the Central Plain. But the most important discovery was a grave measuring about three metres square and containing some large drums and vessels of bronze, a bronze figure of a kneeling woman over a foot high and many ornate bronze daggers and spear-heads. It is believed to be the tomb of a chieftainess of the aboriginal tribes of Yünnan whose conflicts with the imperial armies are recorded in the 2nd and 1st centuries B.C.

The shapes of weapons and socketed axes from this tomb are distinct from those of Chinese tradition and their geometric and figured ornament owes nothing to the characteristic art of central China of the late Chou and Han periods. Like the bronze culture of D'ong-Son in north Annam to which they are more nearly related, the Shih Chai Shan bronzes represent a local tradition of linear and plastic art in which the metal is handled with skill hardly inferior to the highest Chinese standard. The knowledge of metal working must have reached Yünnan from Central China.

In the year 334 B.C. King Ch'ing Hsiang of the southern state of Ch'u had sent an expedition to the region of the Tien Ch'ih lake under General Chuang Ch'iao. The expeditionaries lingered there until 280 B.C. when their way home was cut off by the forces of Ch'in. Chuang Ch'iao, who is reported as still living, decided to remain permanently in the region, and he founded a state and called himself a king. It is not unreasonable to connect with these events the Chinese influence detectable in the remains discovered at Shih Chai Shan. The date of the latter is, however, much later.

Some bronze mirrors included in the grave goods, of ordinary Chinese types, serve to date the burial to the 1st century B.C.

The ceremonial bronze drums illustrated in Pls. 122 and 123 are similar to drums found throughout South-east Asia, of a shape which was manufactured by Shan tribes in Burma until quite recent times, but they are unique in having the upper surfaces crowded with human figures. On the drum decorated with phoenixes (Pl. 122) there are three figures of men and fifteen of women. One of the latter is seated on a throne at the centre, while others kneel and hold up offerings to her. At the edges are women engaged in plaiting and other unidentifiable tasks. The hair styles of the women, some having several plaits, others with double-coiled buns, resemble those still seen among the Miao women of South-west China at the present time. The other drum-top has 41 people, and 11 others found loose are thought also to have belonged to it. At the centre is a pillar supporting a tiger and entwined with two serpents. An execution scene seems to be in progress, the victim being tied down on a board. Another man is bound kneeling. A woman apparelled like the central figure of the first drum is raised aloft on a seat. Behind the central pillar is a row of seated figures, some holding firewood, others raising baskets filled with fish and other objects. Two drums stand at the edge of the group.

It is surmised that the scene of the first drum illustrates a chieftainess enthroned, and the second a religious rite which includes human sacrifice. The presence of the pillar suggests a connexion with shamanistic cosmology. The modelling of the figures is crude but expressive. The figures of animals and people engraved on the sides of some of the other bronze vessels have greater sophistication. A socketed axe is decorated with the design of a human head which appears to be decorated according to the custom of head-hunters.

Ref.: *K'ao Ku Hsüeh Pao*, 1956.1.43.

The Palaeolithic and Neolithic Periods

1. General view of river terrace in loess at Ting Ts'un, Shansi Province.

2. Excavations in progress at Ting Ts'un, Shansi Province.

3. ANIMAL BONES IN SITU IN THE GRAVEL AT TING TS'UN, Shansi Province.

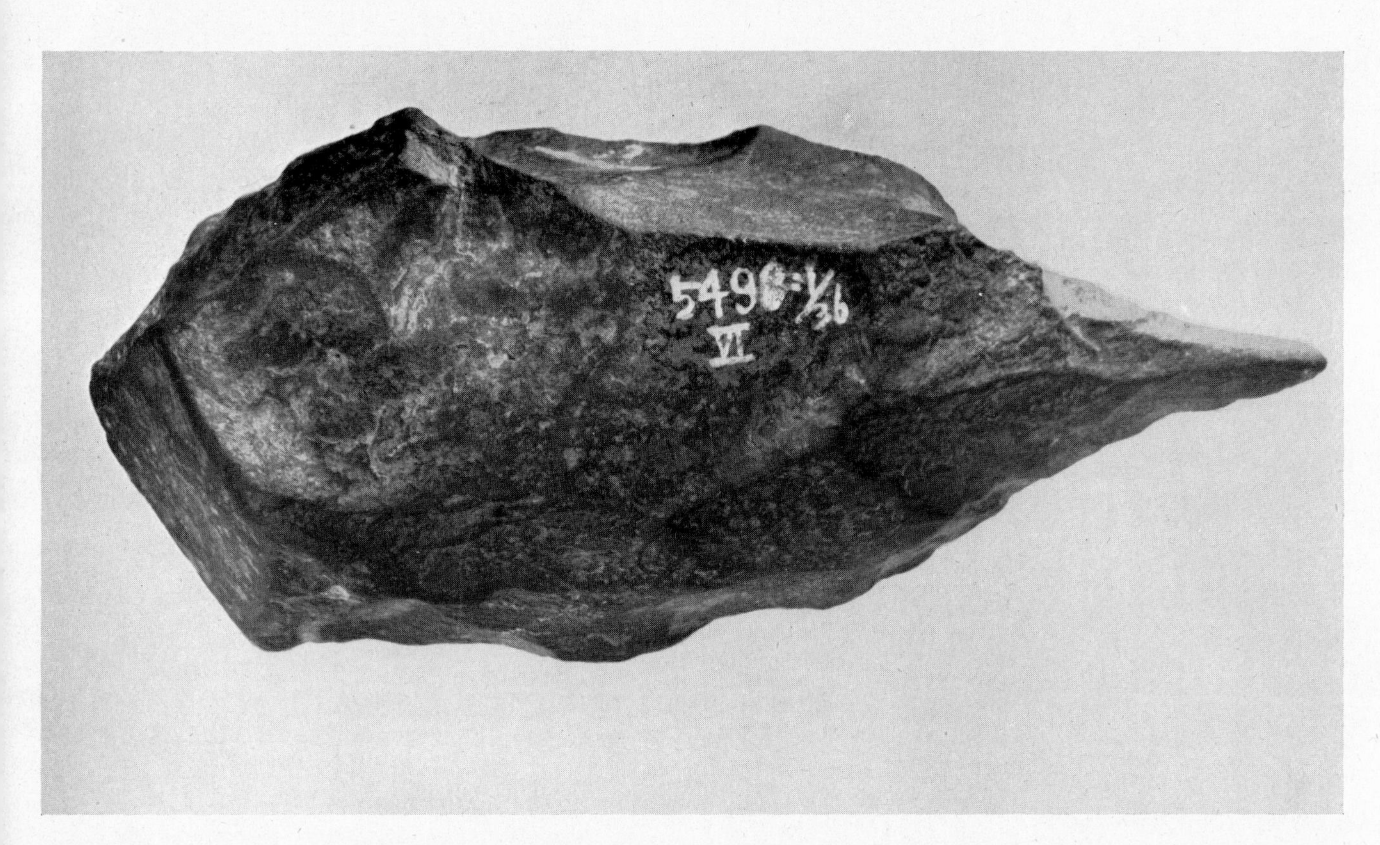

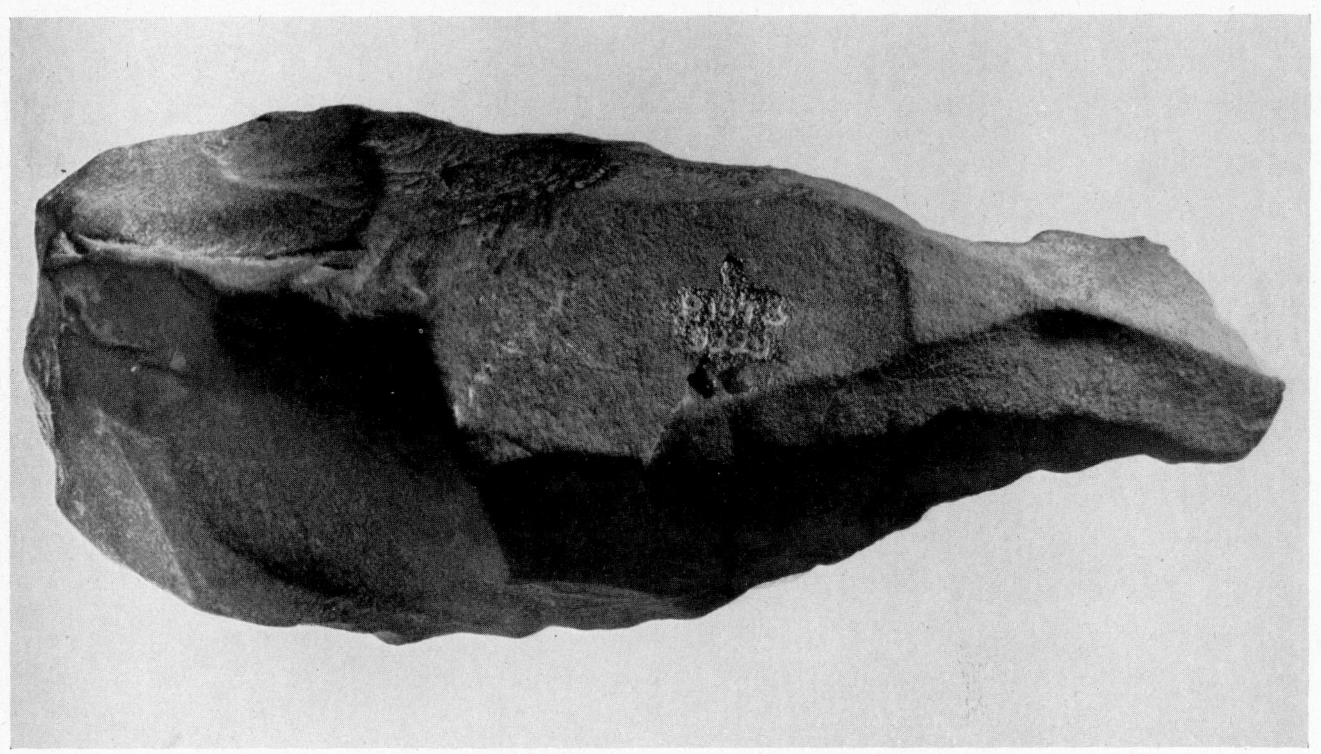

4. Pointed stone implements of 'hand-axe' type. Ting Ts'un, Shansi Province.

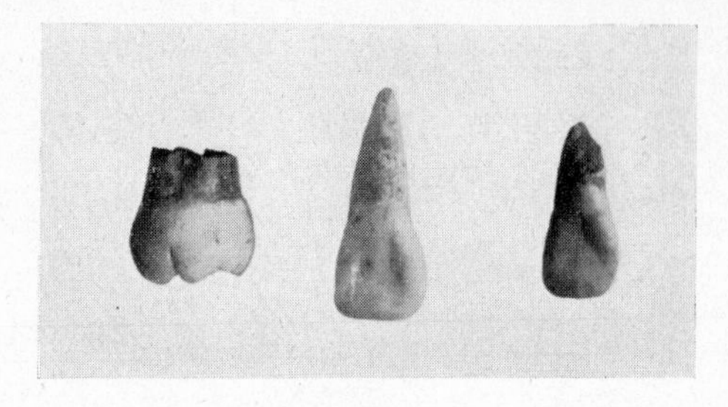

5c. Human teeth.
Ting Ts'un, Shansi Province.

5a, b. Stone tools made of flakes with one edge trimmed. Ting Ts'un, Shansi Province.

6a. GENERAL VIEW OF EXCAVATIONS AT PAN PO TS'UN NEOLITHIC VILLAGE, Shensi Province.

6b. HOUSE FOUNDATION WITH INTERNAL STRUCTURES FORMED IN THE EARTH. Pan Po Ts'un, Shensi Province.

7. HUT FOUNDATIONS WITH POST-HOLES AND REMAINS OF ROOFING CLAY. Pan Po Ts'un, Shensi Province. Diam. about 5 metres.

8. GRAIN STORAGE PITS. Pan Po Ts'un, Shensi Province.

9a. Red pottery bowl with decoration in black. Pan Po Ts'un, Shensi Province. Diam. 38 cms.

9b. Fragments of painted yang-shao ware from Pan Po Ts'un, Shensi Province. British Museum. Length of fragment at top left, 11 cms.

10a. RED POTTERY AMPHORA.
Pan Po Ts'un, Shensi Province.
Ht 31 cms. British Museum.

10b. RED POTTERY BOWL from
Pan Po Ts'un, Shensi Province.
Ht 10·5 cms. British Museum.

11. NEOLITHIC GRAVE EXCAVATED. Pai Tao Kou P'ing, Kansu Province.

12. Red pottery cup. Pai Tao Kou P'ing, Kansu Province. Ht 10·5 cms.

13. Funeral urn decorated in black and red. Pai Tao Kou P'ing, Kansu Province. Ht 22 cms.

14. AMPHORA DECORATED IN BLACK AND RED. Pai Tao Kou P'ing, Kansu Province. Ht 13·7 cms.

15. AMPHORA DECORATED IN BLACK AND RED. Pai Tao Kou P'ing, Kansu Province. Ht 15 cms.

16a. Amphora decorated in black and red. Pai Tao Kou P'ing, Kansu Province. Ht. 10 cms.

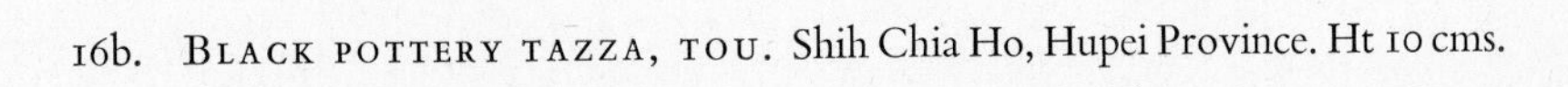

16b. Black pottery tazza, tou. Shih Chia Ho, Hupei Province. Ht 10 cms.

17a. STONE KNIFE. Shih Chia Ho, Hupei Province. Length 12 cms.

17b. STONE AXE. Shih Chia Ho, Hupei Province. Length 15·8 cms.

18a. Red pottery bowl with incised t'ao t'ieh. Shih Chia Ho, Hupei Province. Ht 5·3 cms.

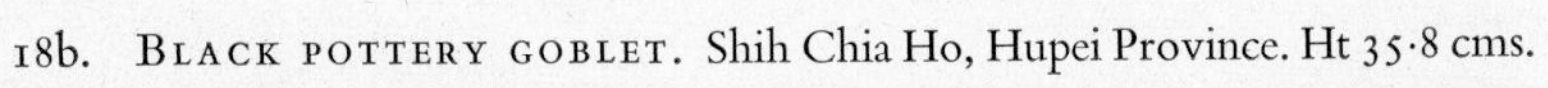

18b. Black pottery goblet. Shih Chia Ho, Hupei Province. Ht 35·8 cms.

19a. GREY POTTERY VASE. Shih Chia Ho, Hupei Province. Ht 18·5 cms.

19b. RED POTTERY JAR. Shih Chia Ho, Hupei Province. Ht 61 cms.

20. GREY POTTERY TRIPOD VESSEL TING. Shih Chia Ho, Hupei Pro vince. Ht 28·5 cms.

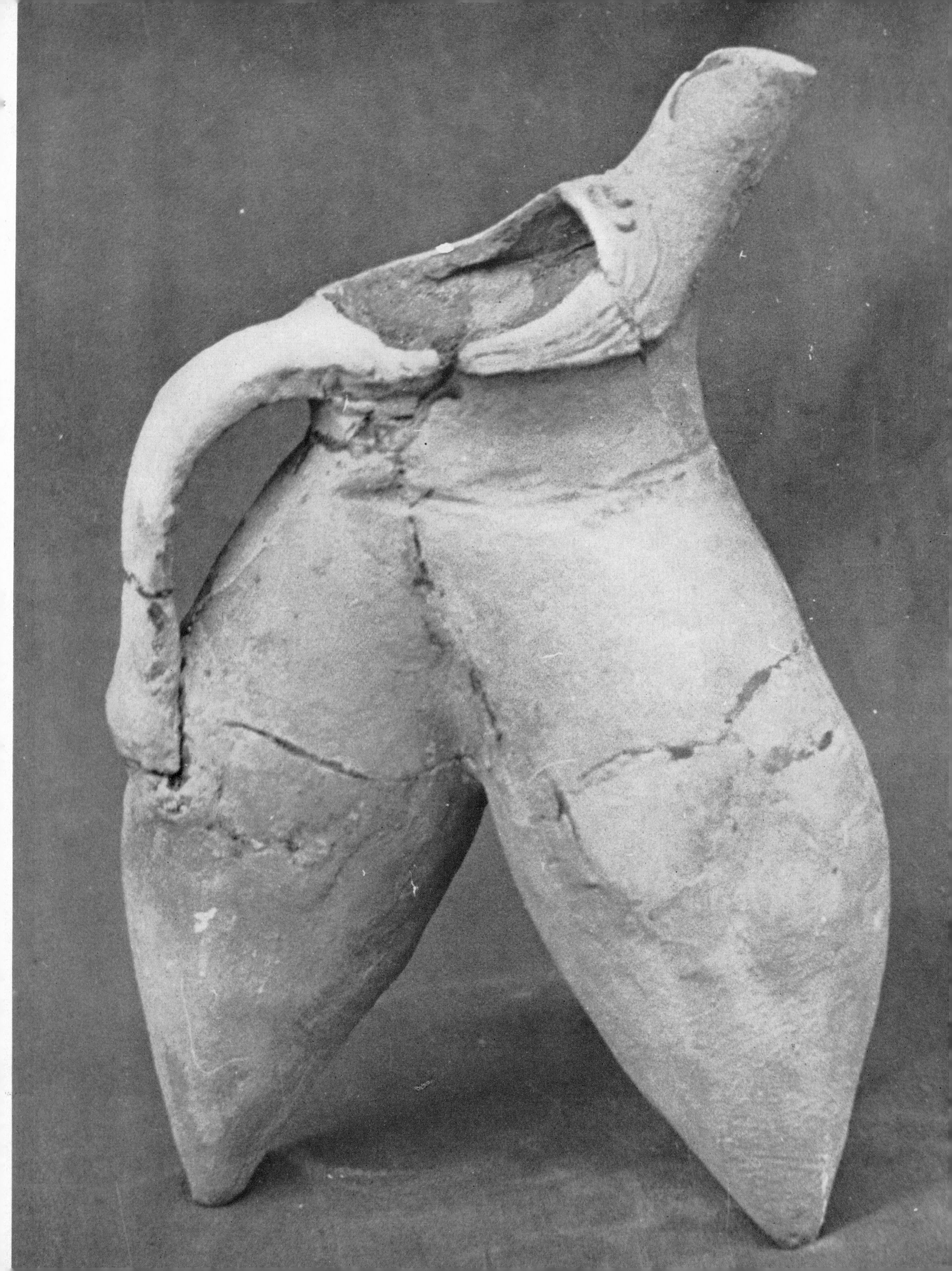

22. Red pottery vase on high foot. Hua T'ing Ts'un, Kiangsu Province. Ht 27·3 cms.

21. Red pottery three-lobed jug, k'uei.
Shih Chia Ho, Hupei Province. Ht 18·4 cms.

23. Red pottery jug. Hua T'ing Ts'un, Kiangsu Province. Ht 20 cms.

24. Red pottery ting. Hua T'ing Ts'un, Kiangsu Province. Ht 37·3 cms.

25. STONE AXES. Hua T'ing Ts'un, Kiangsu Province. Length 19·5 cms. and 22 cms.

26. Red pottery jug. Hua T'ing Ts'un, Kiangsu Province. Ht 25 cms.

27. Black pottery vase. Liang Chu, Chekiang Province. Ht 11·6 cms.

28. BLACK POTTERY PEDESTAL BOWL. Liang Chu, Chekiang Province. Ht 14·7 cms.

29a. Black pottery vase. Liang Chu, Chekiang Province. Ht 12 cms.

29b. Black pottery bowl. Liang Chu, Chekiang Province. Diam. 20 cms.

30. BLACK POTTERY VASE. Liang Chu, Chekiang Province. Ht 14 cms.

31. Black pottery bowl. Liang Chu, Chekiang Province. Ht 10·7 cms.

32a. STONE AXES AND ARROW-HEADS from T'an Shih Shan, Min Hou Hsien, Fukien Province.

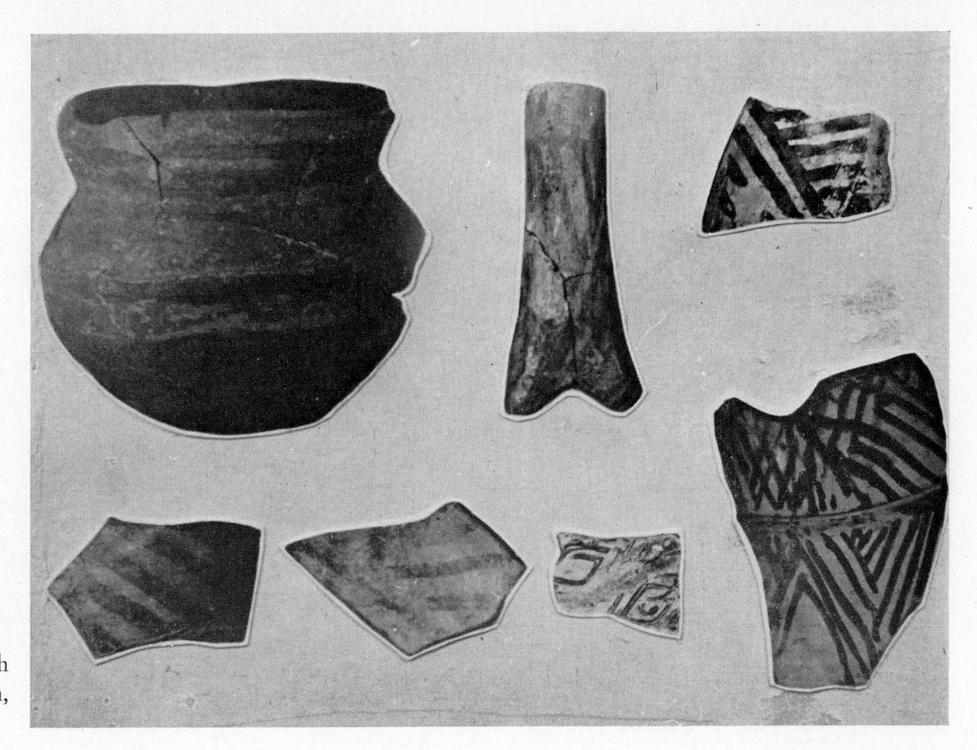

32b. POTTERY from T'an Shih Shan, Min Hou Hsien, Fukien Province.

33a. BLACK POTTERY VASE, the handle missing. From a site of the Lung Shan culture at Jih Chao, Shantung Province. British Museum.

33b. STONE AXES: (*left*) from Lung Shan culture site at Jih Chao, Shantung Province; (*centre and right*) from a site of the Yang-shao culture at Pu Chao Chai, Honan Province. British Museum.

BRONZE AGE I

The Shang Dynasty

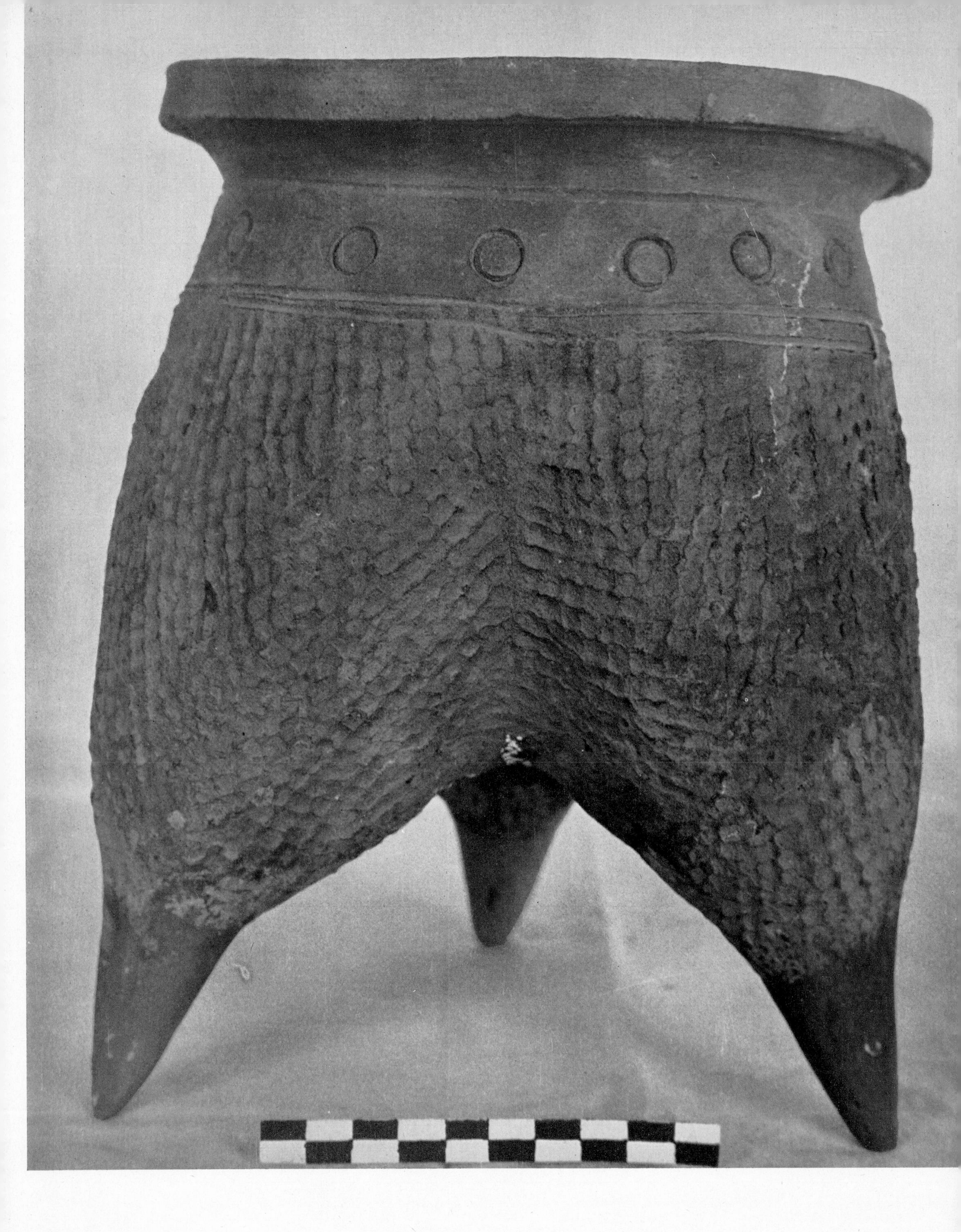

35a. GREY POTTERY TING. Erh Li Kang, Cheng Chou, Honan Province. Ht 16 cms.

35b. GREY POTTERY LI with handle. Erh Li Kang, Cheng Chou, Honan Province. Ht 24 cms.

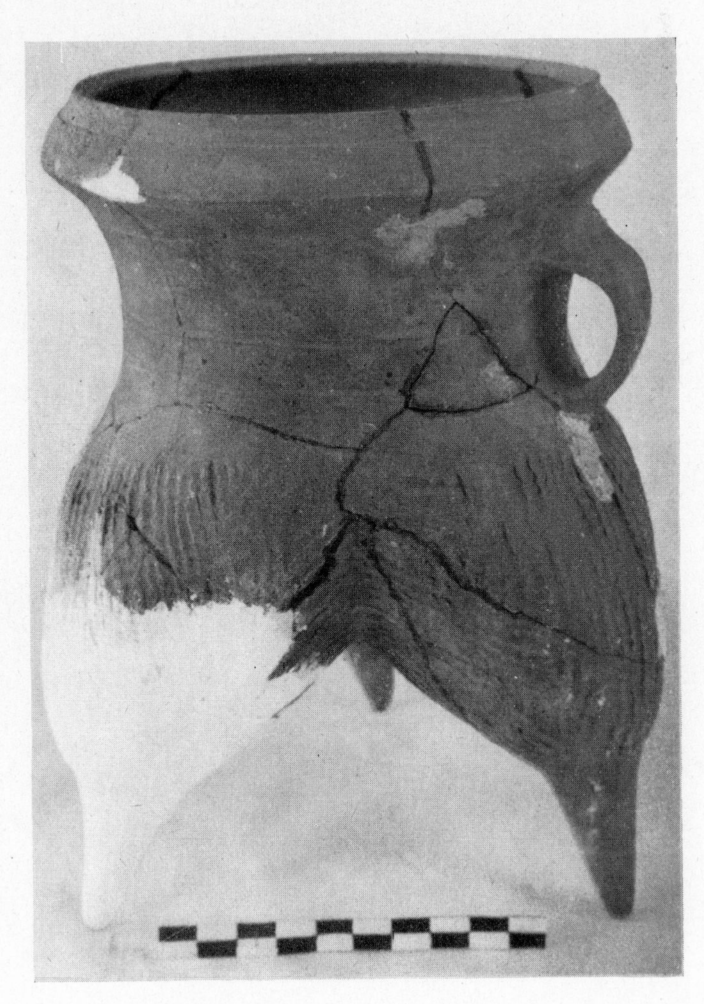

GREY POTTERY LI. Erh Li Kang, Cheng Chou, Honan Province. Ht 25 cms.

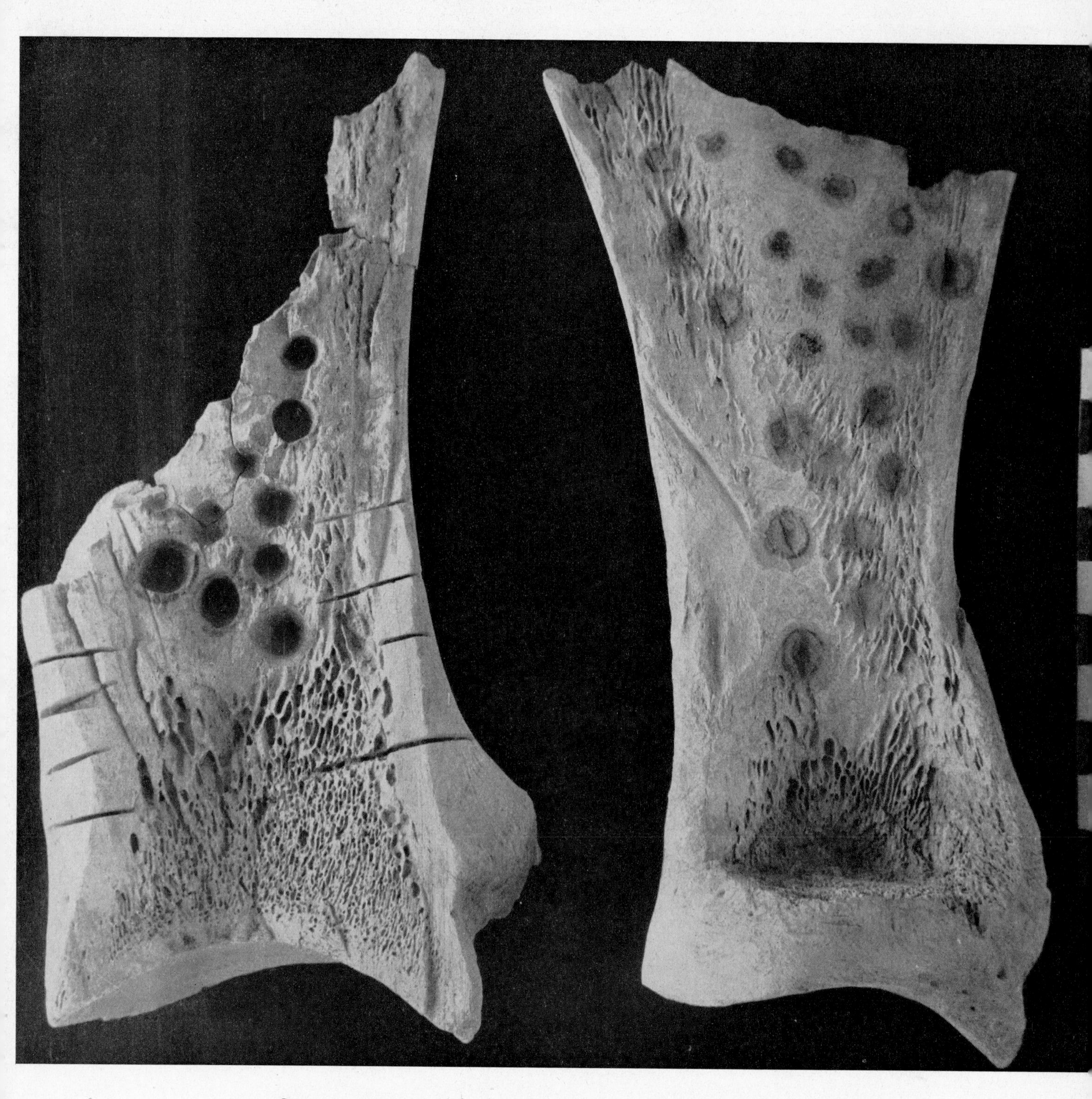

36. ORACLE BONE. A scapula of an ox, showing the pitting and burns made in taking an oracle. Erh Li Kang, Cheng Chou, Honan Province. Ht *c.* 15 cms.

37. Dark grey pottery bowl. Erh Li Kang, Cheng Chou, Honan Province. Ht 31 cms.

38. Ivory goblet. Erh Li Kang, Cheng Chou, Honan Province. Ht 18·2 cms.

39 GREY POTTERY VASE. Erh Li Kang, Cheng Chou, Honan Province. Ht 36 cms.

40. GREY POTTERY GOBLET. Erh Li Kang, Cheng Chou, Honan Province. Ht 19·3 cms.

41. BRONZE LI. Liu Li Ko, Hui Hsien
Honan Province. Ht 20 cms.

43. CHÜEH. Liu Li Ko, Hui Hsien, Honan Province. Ht 25 cms.

42. BRONZE CHIA. Liu Li Ko, Hui Hsien, Honan Province. Ht 24 cms.

4. BRONZE KU. Liu Li Ko, Hui Hsien, Honan Province. Ht 18 cms.

45. PRONE BURIAL IN STEPPED PIT, WITH GRAVE GOODS. Ta Ssŭ K'ung Ts'un, Anyang, Honan Province.

47. Bronze sheathing from yoke. Ta Ssŭ K'ung Ts'un, Anyang, Honan Province. Ht 63 cms.

. Chariot burial. Ta Ssŭ K'ung Ts'un, Anyang, Honan Province. Length of main beam 3.8 metres.

48. Bronze bow-shaped mounts with terminal jingles. Length 45 cms. Bronze knife. Length 29 cms. Bone ornament. Length 13 cms. Ta Ssŭ K'ung Ts'un, Anyang, Honan Province.

49. BRONZE HARNESS MOUNTS. The triangular mount on the left is intended for the horse's forehead; length 15·2 cms. Ta Ssŭ K'ung Ts'un, Anyang, Honan Province.

50. Bronze wine-vessel, yu, in the shape of addorsed birds. Ht 33 cms. Ta Ssŭ K'ung Ts'un, Anyang, Honan Province.

51. Grey pottery goblet with incised pattern. Ht 25 cms. Ta Ssŭ K'ung Ts'un, Anyang, Honan Province.

53. Bronze pole finial with human and animal masks. Shang Dynasty. Ht 15 cms. British Museum.

2. Bronze goblet, ku. Ht 35 cms. Ta Ssŭ K'ung Ts'un, Anyang, Honan Province.

55. Musical stone from the great tomb at Wu Kuan Ts'un, Anyang, Honan Province. Length 81 cms.

54. Central pit of the great tomb at Wu Kuan Ts'un, Anyang, Honan Province. Mouth of central pit 14 by 12 metres.

56. Bronze ritual tripod vessel, ting. Shang Dynasty. Ht 20·5 cms. British Museum.

BRONZE AGE II

The Earlier Chou Dynasty

57. BRONZE WINE-VESSEL, YU. Hai Tao Ying Tzŭ, Jehol Province. Ht 24.6 cms.

58. BRONZE STEAMER, HSIEN. Hai Ta
Ying Tzŭ, Jehol Province. Ht 44·6 cm

59. Bronze water-vessel, p'an. Hai Tao Ying Tzŭ, Jehol Province. Width 33 cms.

60. BRONZE FOOD-VESSEL, KUEI. Hai Tao Ying Tzŭ, Jehol Province. Ht 16·8 cms.

61. Bronze food-vessel, yü. Hai Tao Ying Tzŭ, Jehol Province.

62. Bronze food-vessel, ting. Hai Tao Ying Tzŭ, Jehol Province. Ht 23·5 cms.

63a. BRONZE FOOD-VESSEL, YÜ. Yen Tun Shan, Kiangsu Province. Ht 12 cms.

63b. BRONZE FOOD-VESSEL, THE NIEH KUEI. Yen Tun Shan, Kiangsu Province. Ht 15·7 cms.

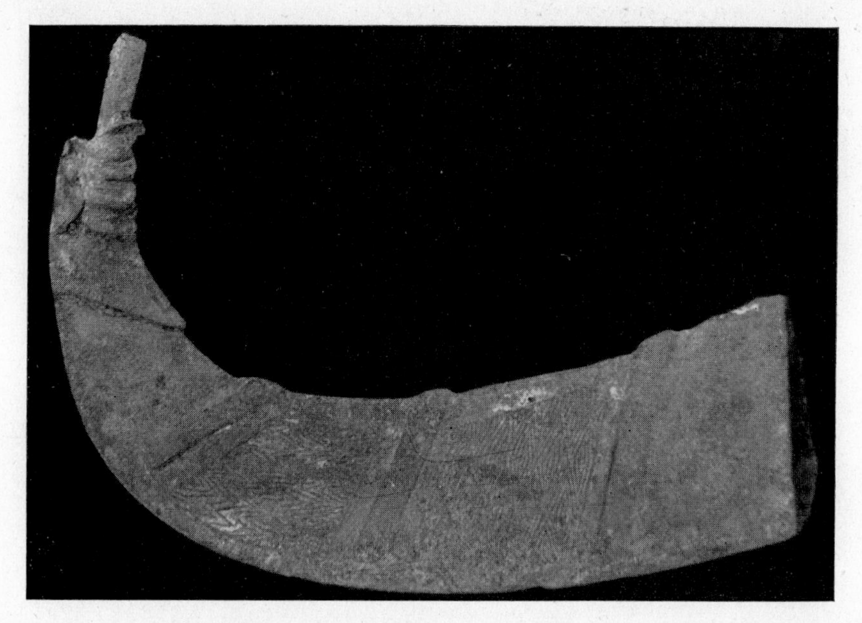

64a. BRONZE HORN-SHAPED DRINKING CUP. Yen Tun Shan, Kiangsu Province. Length 2·58 cms.

64b. BRONZE WATER-VESSEL, P'AN. Yen Tun Shan, Kiangsu Province. Ht 20 cms.

65. BRONZE WINE-VESSEL, KUANG. Yen Tun Shan, Kiangsu Province. Ht 21·1 cms.

66. BRONZE WINE-VESSEL, HO. Yen Tu
Shan, Kiangsu Province. Ht 30·5 cms.

7. BRONZE BELL, CHUNG. P'u Tu Ts'un, Shensi Province. Ht 44 cms.

68. BRONZE WINE-VESSEL, LEI. P'u Tu Ts'un, Shensi Province. Ht 24·8 cms.

69. Wine ewer, ho. P'u Tu Ts'un, Shensi Province. Ht 27·6 cms.

BRONZE AGE III

The Later Chou Dynasty

ɔ.

ʒRONZE BELL, CHUNG.
)ne of a set of nine. Tomb
f the Marquis of Ts'ai, Shou
Isien, Anhwei Province.
It 27 cms.

71.

BRONZE WINE VASE, HU.
From the tomb of the Marquis
of Ts'ai, Shou Hsien, Anhwei
Province. Ht 81 cms.

72. BRONZE STAND. Tomb of the Marquis of Ts'ai, Shou Hsien, Anhwei Province. Ht 22 cms.

73. Bronze bowl, chien. Tomb of the Marquis of Ts'ai, Shou Hsien, Anhwei Province. Ht 85 cms.

74. Bronze food-vessel, tui. Tomb of the Marquis of Ts'ai, Shou Hsien, Anhwei Province. Ht 33 cms.

75. BRONZE FOOD-VESSEL, KUEI. Tomb of the Marquis of Ts'ai, Shou Hsien, Anhwei Province. Ht 36 cms.

76. Bronze food-vessel. Tomb of the Marquis of Ts'ai, Shou Hsien, Anhwei Province. Ht 52 cms.

77. BRONZE WATER-VESSEL. Tomb of the Marquis of Ts'ai, Shou Hsien, Anhwei Province. Ht 36 cms.

78a, b. IRON MOULD FOR CASTING BRONZE AXES. Hsing Lung Hsien, Jehol Province. Length 29·2 cms.

79. EARTH FORMS OF CHARIOTS. Liu Li Ko, Hui Hsien, Honan Province.

80. BRONZE HU. Chao Ku, Hui Hsien, Honan Province. Ht (inc. handle) 37·8 cms.

81. BRONZE STEAMER, HSIEN. Chao Ku
Hui Hsien, Honan Province. Ht 60 cms

82a. GLASS BEADS. Ku Wei Ts'un, Hui Hsien, Honan Province. Diam. of the largest bead, 2·3 cms. From left to right in the top row the colours are black, blue, green, blue and white on green, blue. The remainder have blue spots outlined in white on a green body.

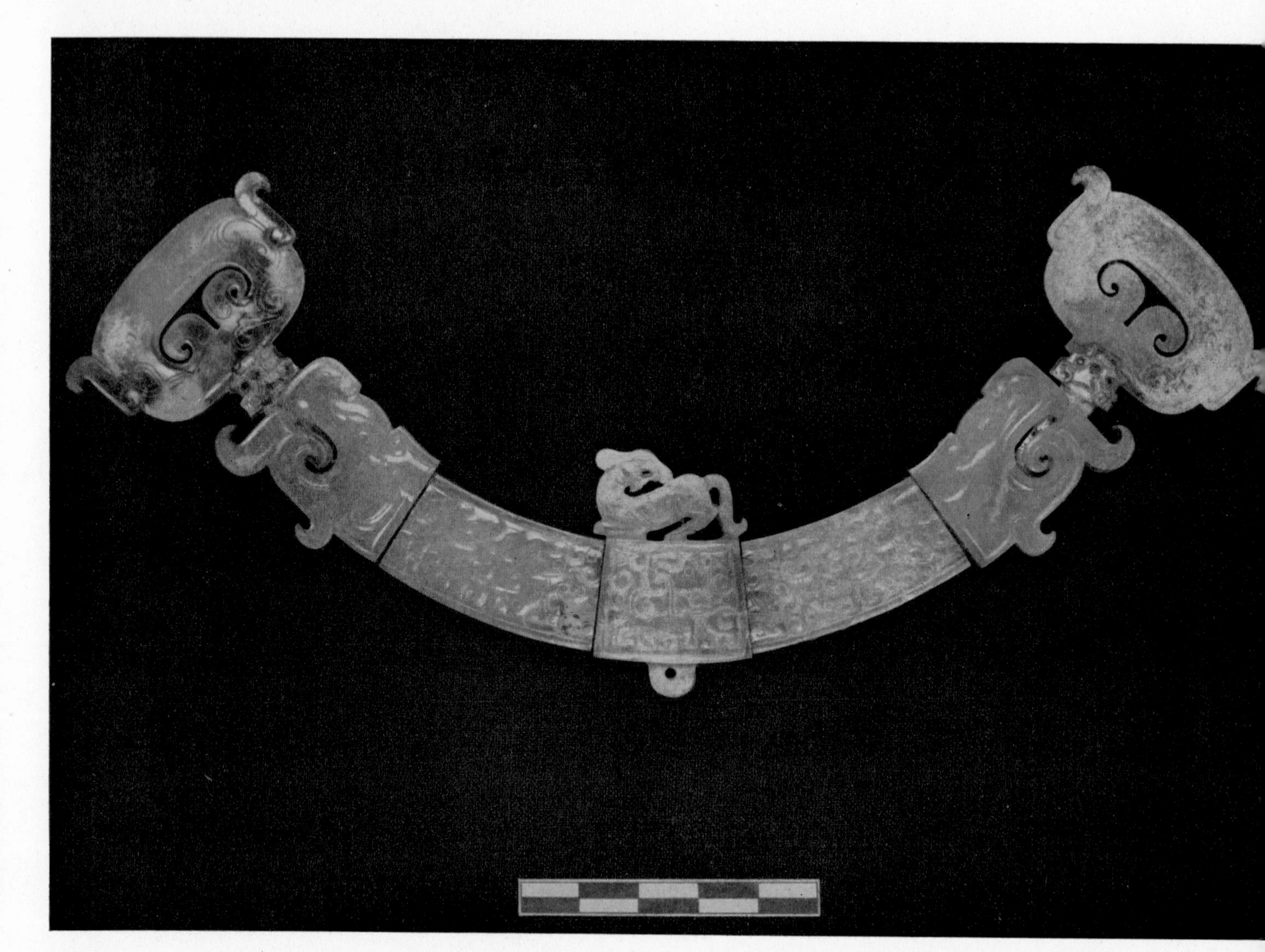

82b. JADE PENDANT, in seven parts, with two gilt bronze tiger masks. Ku Wei Ts'un, Hui Hsien, Honan Province. Length 20·2 cms.

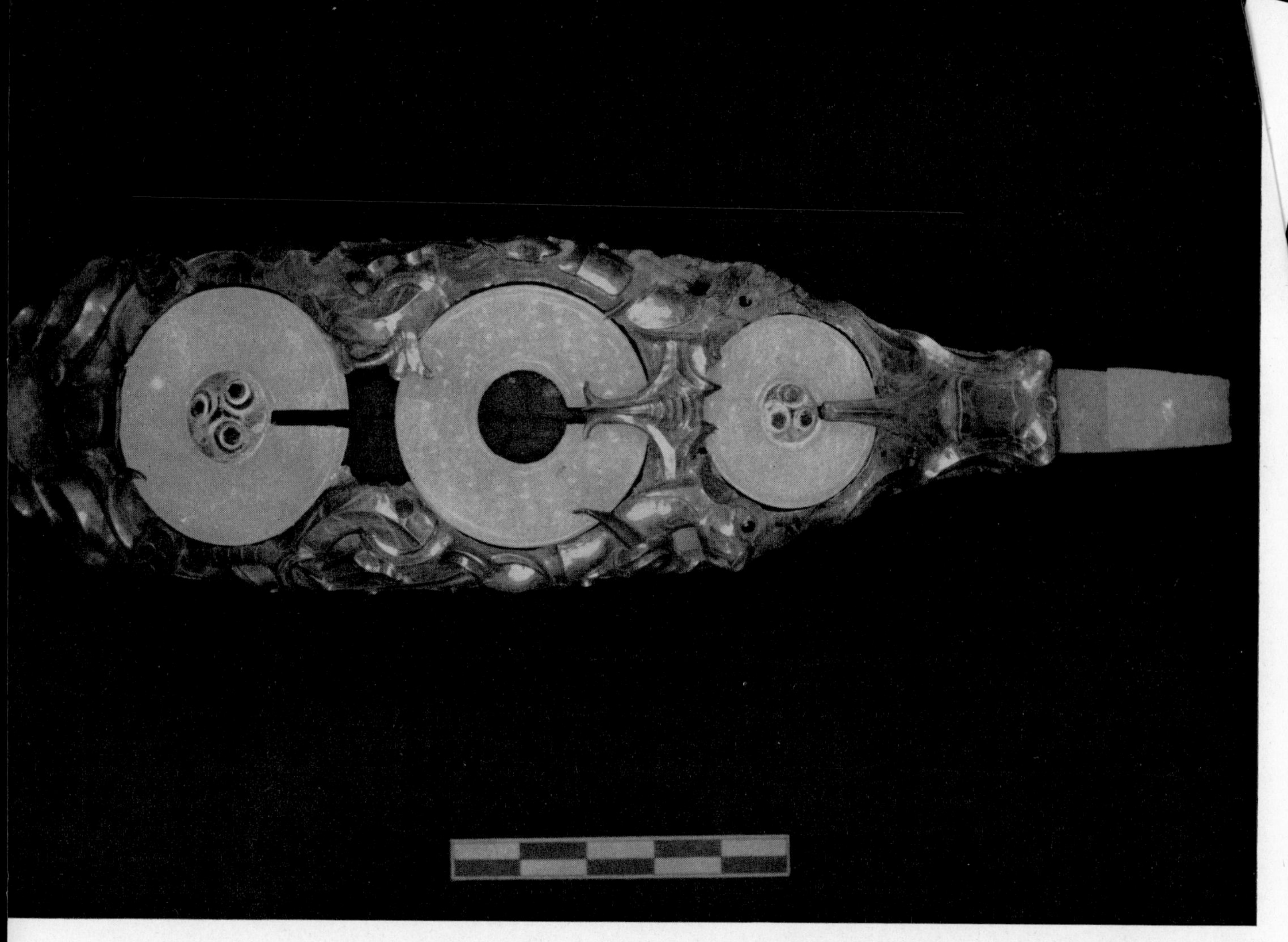

83a. SILVER GILT BELT-HOOK with jade and glass inlay. Ku Wei Ts'un, Hui Hsien, Honan Province. Length 18·4 cms.

83b. HUMAN FIGURE AND GRIFFIN-LIKE ORNAMENT OF GREENISH JADE. Ku Wei Ts'un, Hui Hsien, Honan Province. Ht 4·3 cms. and 7·5 cms.

84a, b. IRON IMPLEMENTS. (*a*) spade-edge; (*b*) hoe blades. Ku Wei Ts'un, Hui Hsien, Honan Province. Width of spade edge 23 cm

85. BRONZE FOOD-VESSEL, TOU. Chia Ko Chuang, T'ang Shan, Hopei Province. Ht 35·3 cm

87. BRONZE WATER-VESSEL, YI. Chia Ko Chuang, T'ang Shan, Hopei Province. Ht 16 cms.

BRONZE WINE VASE, HU. Decorated with scenes of hunting. Chia Ko Chuang, T'ang Shan, Hopei Province. Ht 34·9 cms.

88. Bronze food-vessel, tui. Chia Ko Chuang, T'ang Shan, Hopei Province. Ht 22 cms.

The Han Period

89a. LACQUERED TOILET BOX. Ch'ang Sha, Hunan Province. Diam. 21 cms.

89b. BODY WRAPPED IN A GRASS MAT. Ch'ang Sha, Hunan Province.

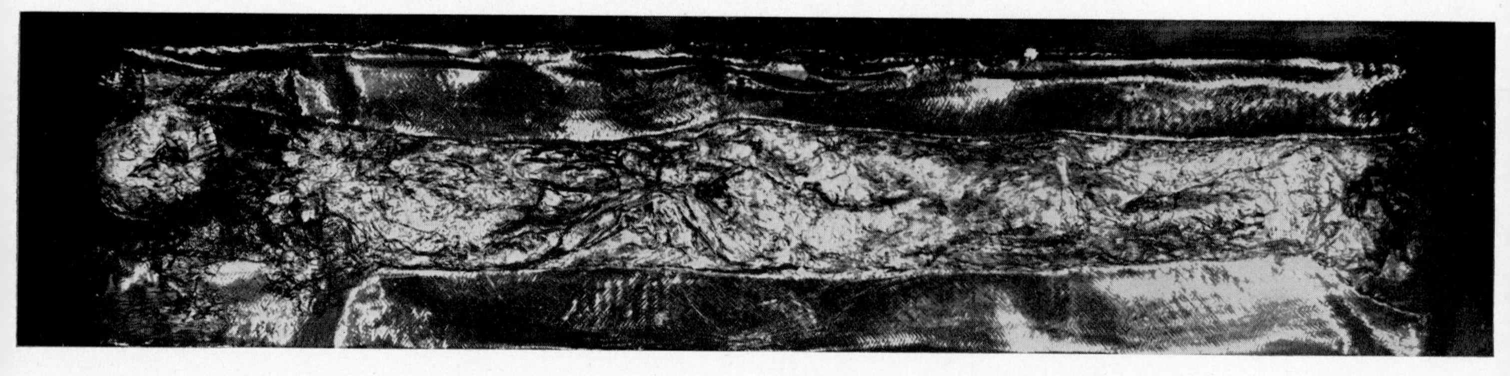

90. CONTENTS OF A LACQUERED TOILET BOX. Ch'ang Sha, Hunan Province.

91. Lacquered wine cup. Ch'ang Sha, Hunan Province. Length 16·5 cms.

92. WOODEN BOARD OF A MUSICAL INSTRUMENT, CH'IN. Ch'ang Sha, Hunan Province. Length 180 cms.

93. Pair of lacquer wine cups. Ch'an Sha, Hunan Provinc Length 16·5 cms.

94. CONTENTS OF A LACQUERED TOILET BOX, including two smaller boxes, combs, pins and a bronze knife-handle. Ch'ang Sha, Hunan Province.

95. Lacquered toilet box. Ch'ang Sha, Hunan Province. Diam. 32·8 cms.

96. Lacquered toilet box with bronze mounts. Ch'ang Sha, Hunan Province. Ht 17·7 cms

97. Wooden grave figures. Ch'ang Sha, Hunan Province. Ht 52, 55 cms.

98. Middle chamber of the tomb, looking towards the entrance to a side chamber on the west side. Wang Tu, Hopei Provinc

99. ANTECHAMBER OF THE TOMB WITH MURALS OF GATE SENTINELS, looking towards the stone gates leading to the interior. Wang Tu, Hopei Province.

100. PAINTINGS ON THE WALLS OF THE ANTECHAMBER TO THE TOMB: (*a*) west wall; (*b*, *c*) east wall. Wang Tu, Hopei Province.

The next four plates show details of the paintings.

101. AN OFFICIAL BOWING TOWARDS THE DEAD.
102. AN OFFICIAL BOWING TOWARDS THE DEAD.
103. OFFICIALS OF THE CARRIAGE SERVICE.
104. AN OFFICIAL BOWING TOWARDS THE DEAD.

下功曹

門下小史

車伍佰人

曹

105. MURAL PAINTING OF THE WHITE MOON HARE. Wang Tu, Hopei Province.

106a. Pottery model with figures and pond. Hsin Tsao Hsiang, Mien Yang Hsien, Szechwan Province. Length 49·5 cms.

106b. Pottery figure of a musician. Hsin Tsao Hsiang, Mien Yang Hsien, Szechwan Province. Ht 30 cms.

108. Pottery figure of an attendant. Hsin Tsao Hsiang, Mien Yang Hsien, Szechwan Province. Ht 33 cms.

Pottery figure of a dancer. Hsin Tsao Hsiang, Mien Yang Hsien, Szechwan Province. Ht 47·5 cms.

109. POTTERY FIGURE OF AN ATTENDANT. Hsin Tsao Hsiang, Mien Yang Hsien, Szechwan Province. Ht 31·4 cms.

110a. Boat-shaped capital with side brackets in the shape of dragon heads. Pei Chai Ts'un, Shantung Province.

110b. Entrance, south-facing, of the tomb. Pei Chai Ts'un, Shantung Province. Ht of lintel, 1·44 metres.

111. DETAIL OF MIDDLE PILLAR OF THE TOMB. Pei Chai Ts'un, Shantung Province.

112. DETAIL OF RIGHT-HAND PILLAR OF THE TOMB.
Pei Chai Ts'un,
Shantung Province.

113.
Octagonal pillar in the first chamber of the tomb.
Pei Chai Ts'un, Shantung Province.

114
Roof with corbelling and coffers in the east bay of the rear chambe[r] of the tomb.
Pei Chai Ts'un, Shantung Province.

116a. Lacquer from the side of a box, decorated with a tiger and a 'feathered man'. Lung Sheng Kang, Kuangtung Province.

116b. Remains of a lacquered shield with figure of the hero Ch'ih Yu. Lung Sheng Kang, Kuangtung Province.

115a.

Lacquer plaque decorated with crane in clouds. Lung Sheng Kang, Kuangtung Province.

115b.

Lacquer plaque decorated with figure of the hero Ch'ih Yu. Lung Sheng Kang, Kuangtung Province.

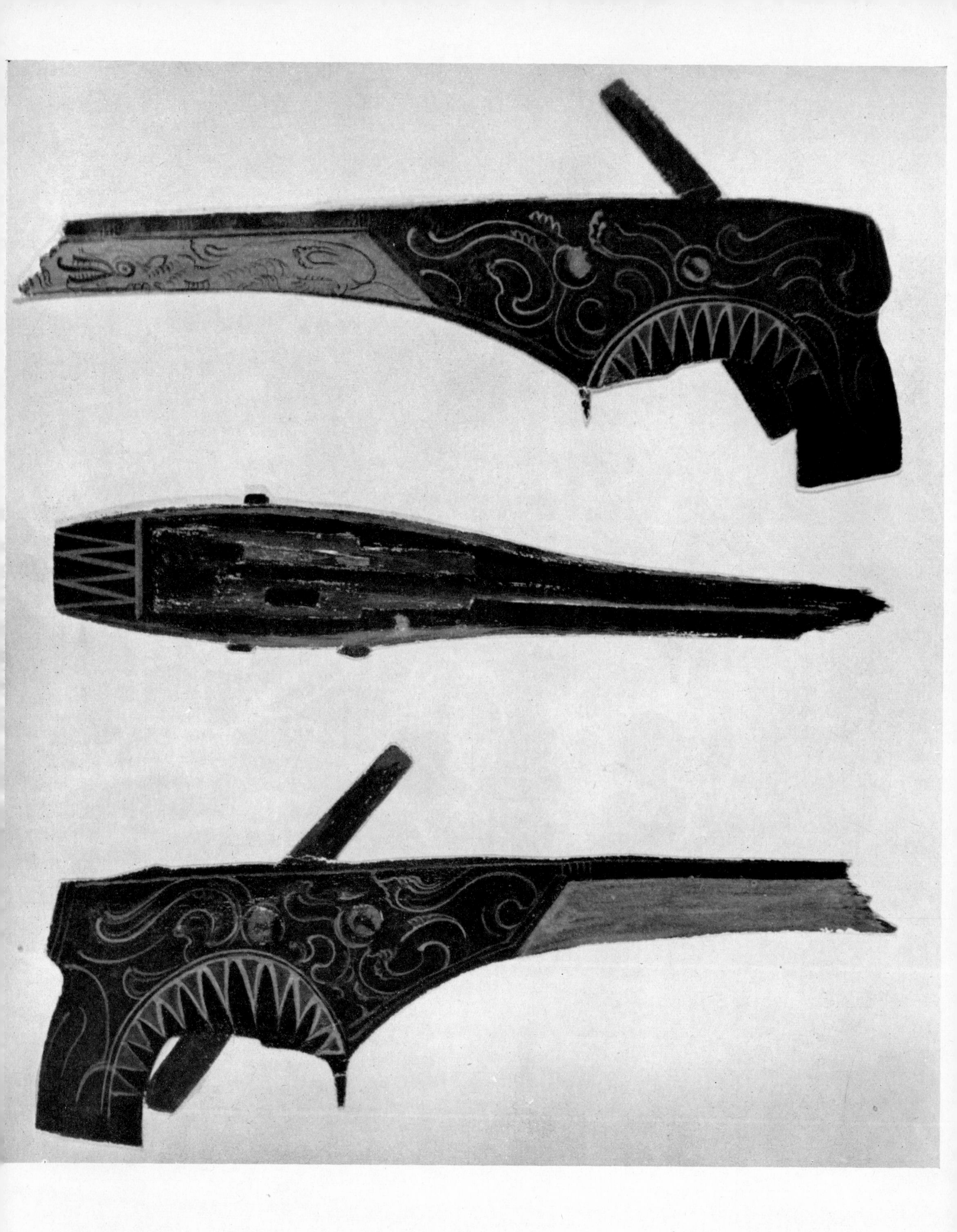

118. FLOOR OF A HOUSE. Western suburb of Loyang, Honan Province.

.17. THREE VIEWS OF LACQUERED WOODEN STOCK OF A CROSS-BOW.
Lung Sheng Kang, Kuangtung Province. Remaining length 22·4 cms.

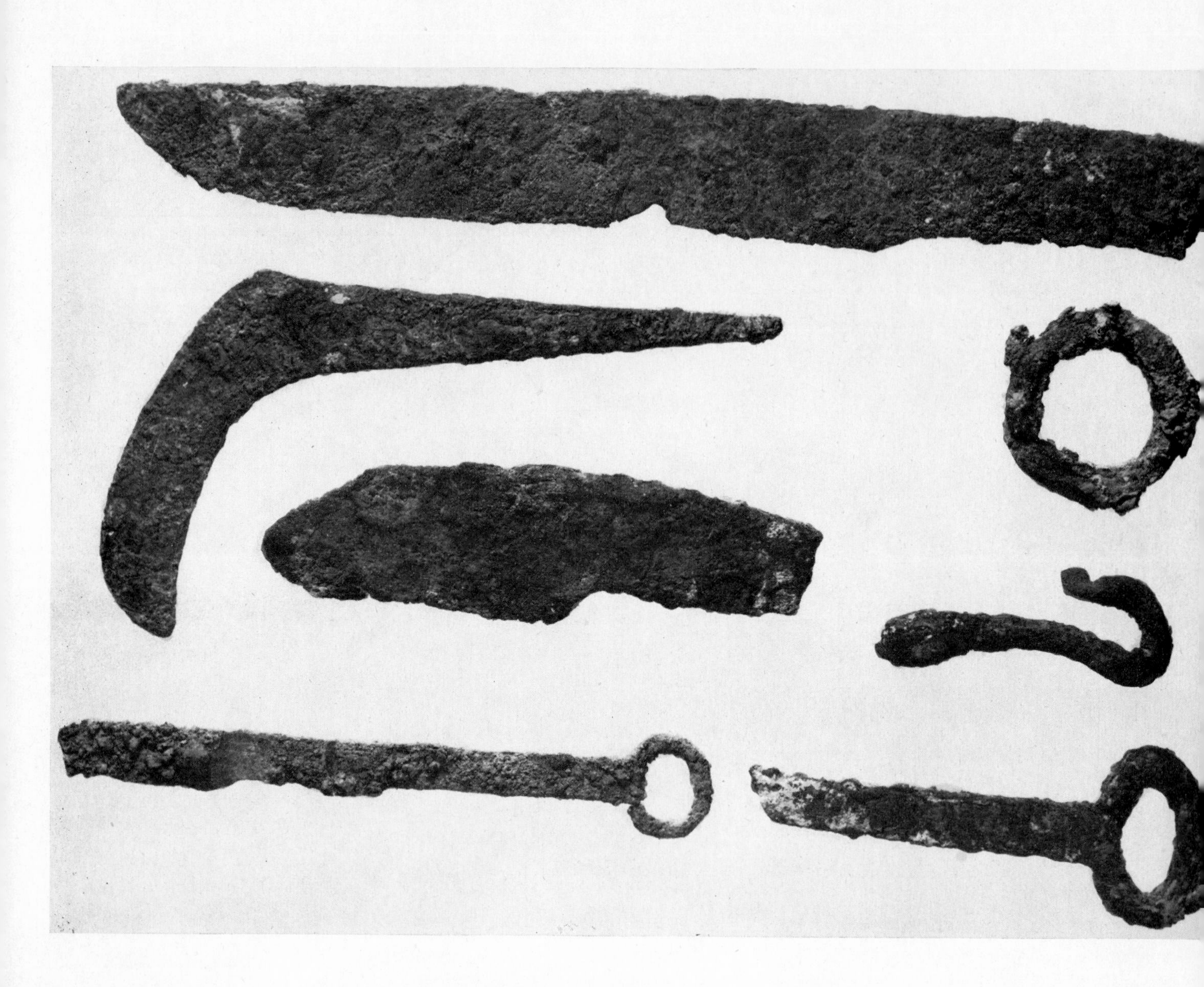

119. Iron knives and sickles, ring and belt-hook. Western Suburb of Loyang, Honan Province.

120. Clay model of a walled house, from a brick tomb in the Eastern Suburb of Canton. Ht about 35 cms.

121. Clay model of a boat, from a brick tomb in the Eastern Suburb of Canton. Length 54 cms.

122. Bronze ceremonial drum with scene of chieftainess enthroned.
Shih Chai Shan, Chin Ning Hsien, Yü nan Province. Diam. of top 25 cms.

123. Bronze ceremonial drum with scene of religious rite.
Shih Chai Shan, Chin Ning Hsien, Yünnan Province. Diam. of top 30 cms.